Secret Societies

Opus Dei

Catholicism's Secret Sect

Conrad Bauer

Copyrights

All rights reserved. © Conrad Bauer and Maplewood Publishing No part of this publication or the information in it may be quoted from or reproduced in any form by means such as printing, scanning, photocopying, or otherwise without prior written permission of the copyright holder.

Disclaimer and Terms of Use

Effort has been made to ensure that the information in this book is accurate and complete. However, the author and the publisher do not warrant the accuracy of the information, text, and graphics contained within the book due to the rapidly changing nature of science, research, known and unknown facts, and internet. The author and the publisher do not hold any responsibility for errors, omissions, or contrary interpretation of the subject matter herein. This book is presented solely for motivational and informational purposes only. The publisher and author of this book does not control or direct users' actions and are not responsible for the information or content shared, harm and/or action of the book readers. The presentation of the information is without contract or any type of guarantee assurance. This book is not meant to be used, nor should it be used, to diagnose or treat any medical condition. For diagnosis or treatment of any medical problem, consult your own physician. The publisher and author are not responsible for any specific health or allergy needs that may require medical supervision and are not liable for any damages or negative consequences from any treatment, action, application or preparation, to any person reading or following the information in this book. References, if any, are provided for informational purposes only and do not constitute endorsement of any websites or other sources. Readers should be aware that the websites listed in this book, if any, may change.

ISBN: 978-1537250229

Printed in the United States

Contents

Introduction 1
Getting to Know the Work of God 3
Joining Opus Dei 13
A Global Concern 29
Controversy Reigns 55
    Cloaked in Secrecy 55
    Pain Threshold 62
    Women's Place 75
    Follow the Money 81
    The Church and the Government 85
    Is Opus Dei a Cult? 91
Conclusion 97
Further Reading 99
Image Credits 101
About the Author 103
    More Books from Conrad Bauer 104

Introduction

Of the billion or so Catholics in the world, the members of Opus Dei constitute almost a hundredth of one percent. Though their numbers might be relatively minuscule, their reputation is many orders of magnitude greater. While the guiding lights of the Church have taken a more genial, modern approach to religion in the last century, the members of Opus Dei have stuck rigidly to the traditions of old. In doing so, they have become known as the hardcore. The fiercely devoted. The stringently religious. Unmoving, distant, and utterly compelling. In an age when the Vatican is reaching out to many millions of people worldwide, Opus Dei seems to be shrouded in secrecy, a secret sect that adheres to the ancient practices of Christianity.

Perhaps because of this adherence to the older models of Christianity, the group has come to represent the most devoted and most controversial of all Catholic arms. its practices are said to include ancient languages, self-flagellation, corporal mortification, aggressive recruiting, controlling the free will of members, cult-like behavior, misogynistic policies, support of fascists, and many more secrets hidden away within the organization's walls.

In this book, we will attempt to look deeply into the hidden history of Catholicism's most radical and divisive sect. Using ancient texts, accounts of former members, extensive research, and secret documents, we will discover the truth behind Opus Dei. If you would like to learn more about this zealous, sometimes terrifying organization, then read on. For the truth behind Catholicism's secret sect, this book is all you will ever need.

Getting to Know the Work of God

Before we begin our in-depth study of Opus Dei, we should take the time to get a general overview of the organization itself. It is commonly misunderstood, and there are many rumors, conspiracy theories, and superstitions that surround the institution and its practitioners. If we are to discover the truth, then it is important to understand the basics.

The name itself is Latin. Translated, Opus Dei means "Work of God." That gives us an insight into the core belief of the group. That is to say, it is their belief that God is not limited solely to the Church. Instead, one can infuse their own work with a sanctity and a dedication to religion at all times. Whether you're an engineer, a plumber, or a schoolteacher, the work that you carry out as an Opus Dei member is dedicated to God. There is a religious appreciation of the mundane details of life, often giving the appearance of religious fervor that can appear odd to the outsider. Together, the members of the church and its clergy dedicate their lives and their work to the divine power. Literally, the day-to-day lives of members becomes the eponymous work of God.

But Opus Dei is so much more than this. Over time, the group has come to embody long-standing criticisms of Catholicism and the history of organized religion. It has become associated with a biblical literalism and a staunchly conservative mind-set. There have even been suggestions of a global conspiracy network. But how to these ideas relate to the basic principles of Opus Dei?

It is true, certainly, that a traditional problem of Opus Dei has been communicating their message to the layman. Often, the organization focuses on promoting what it is not, rather than what it is. This gives Opus Dei a defensive appearance, which – somewhat paradoxically – leads more people to become even more suspicious than ever before. To find out more about what Opus Dei actually is, let's go back to the very beginning.

The date is October 2nd, 1928. A young Spanish priest named Josemaria Escriva makes a retreat to a secluded monastery in Madrid. Inside the Vincentian institution, he has a vision. The details of the vision seem strange, but Escriva is left with no doubt what he must do. After the experience, he is inspired to create his own organization, an order that would eventually become Opus Dei.

The vision of the Spanish priest was the inspiration for Opus Dei. Josemaria Escriva, the man who would later be regarded as the founder of the organization, would have subsequent visions, in which the further details of God's plan were laid out to him. Part of these visions seemed to give Escriva the general overall idea of Opus Dei, while others were more specific. There should be a dedicated branch for women, there should be an organized body of priests, and many other details that would go on to shape the structure and principles of the church. But these would all come later. According to Escriva himself, the original vision contained the essential elements of Opus Dei.

October the 2nd is a special day. It is a recognized day within the Catholic Church, known as the Feast of the Guardian Angels. It was on this day that Escriva received his vision. His own description of the event remembers that it was a feast day. According to the priest's description of his vision, it was on this day that the "Lord willed" that Opus Dei as a group "might come to be." Furthermore, he went on to describe the vision as one that told him of an organization in which men and women were willing to make a sacrifice of themselves for other people, in order to make sure all of the "ways of man" were divine and that every "upright work" would be suitably sanctified. Even if he did not have the structural backing, it clear to see that Escriva had the central tenants of what would prove to be a controversial interpretation of Catholicism.

It's important that Opus Dei's beginnings are the result of seemingly divine inspiration. Escriva's vision provided him and his followers with a holy mandate, a conviction in the importance of the organization's work. Opus Dei, as such, is an extension of God's will. So much so, in fact, that Escriva himself has denied being the actual founder of the group, instead saying that Opus Dei was "founded in spite of [him]" rather than because of him. The origins of the name itself are equally as parochial, with the group going unnamed before an apparently offhand, random comment from Escriva's confessor struck a chord with the priest. When he asked Escriva how the "work of God" was going, Escriva realized quickly that this was to be the name. As such, members now refer to the Church simply as "the Work."

At a foundational level, there is a simple message to Opus Dei's work. It's the same one that was revealed in the vision and built upon in subsequent decades. That is to say, it is the goal of the members to sanctify the ordinary lives of people by living as taught by the gospels and the Church to the fullest extent possible. This is not too far from the belief that most Catholics would espouse, but the group takes their ideas to a more extreme conclusion that most worshippers.

To sum up their aims, Opus Dei members chose as their symbol a simple circle with a cross inside. The circle – representing the world – is sanctified from within. To the members, the idea of being holy is not something that is limited to the higher-ups of the Catholic Church or to the saints, but it is the potential destiny of every single Christian. It's not just the clergy, the nuns, the priests, the saints, or anyone else associated with the Church who are holy. Instead, it's something that is available to everyone in the world. Together, they can sanctify everybody, just as their logo suggests.

But this idea is not just expressed through the normal, typically religious actions such as praying. Instead, small and mundane parts of day-to-day life can become expressions of worship. In particular, one's work should be devoted to the Lord, whether you're an accountant or a construction worker. This is where the beliefs of the Opus Dei members begin to deviate from the path of the traditional Catholic adherents.

But the work of Escriva did not go unnoticed. As he was setting up his organization, he earned himself many admirers. People saw both the priest and his followers as being necessarily pious. Fans included the late Pope John Paul II, who would later describe the man as being ahead of his time. Giovanni Benelli – once the cardinal of Florence – would go on to have many doctrinal disagreements with Escriva, but he still saw fit to compare him with another founder of a dedicated group of Catholics, Saint Ignatius of Loyola, who founded the Jesuit order in the 16th Century. According to Benelli, Escriva similarly managed to translate contemporary discussions within the Catholic Church into a codified, dedicated organization.

The comparison to the Jesuits is particularly telling. For centuries, the Jesuits were seen as the most learned, the most devout, and the most dedicated branch of the clergy. Though many disagreed with some of their practices – or even their very existence – there were many who saw the Jesuits as being absolutely necessary. For many Catholics, the simple existence of the Jesuits was comforting. It was reassuring to know that there were people on Earth who were suitably dedicated to God, suitably pure enough to preach his word and to investigate the ways in which modern life intersected with theology. To many people, Opus Dei filled a similar niche. As their reputation grew – initially within the Catholic community – they developed their reputation for dedicated religious practice. It is out of this dedication that their more controversial elements began to emerge.

Trying to get a grip of the more theological elements can be tough. For anyone who has studied the intricacies of the Catholic doctrine, there are a number of smaller, more refined points where Opus Dei moves away from mainstream religious thinking. For the majority of people, however, it can be difficult to note the key differences between the majority of Catholic thought and the particular practices of Escriva's organization.

Opus Dei members have, on a number of occasions, attempted to publicly clarify their idiosyncratic beliefs. In 2004, for example, an interview with Fernando Ocariz (at the time, the second-highest ranking member of Opus Dei) made an effort to clarify some of Escriva's teachings. The "universal call to holiness" that defines the organization can be split into two distinct parts: the subjective and the objective. The subjective invites people to sanctification. In other words, anyone – regardless of who they are – is called to become a saint. The objective is part of this, in that it states that everything in the world and every element of the human experience can be used to move someone closer toward becoming a saint. For Opus Dei members, every action and every situation is a chance to move closer towards sainthood.

Typically, most Catholics would see sainthood as being something that is limited to only the most holy people. Looking through the traditional pantheon of saints, they were typically priests, monks, or nuns. But for Opus Dei, this is not a limitation. All members, should they follow the Opus Dei teachings, can become saints in their own right. Borrowing words and phrases from the Bible's famous Song of Songs, Escriva himself sought to find God "in the things that come from outside," that is to say, the general day-to-day minutiae of life and work.

But there was a theological drive on the part of Opus Dei's creator. Escriva is on the record as describing his organization as being an "intravenous injection" directly into the "bloodstream of society." The image is vivid and speaks of how great a shock he saw Opus Dei as causing. Escriva wanted to make his group different from the common views of the church, and even in the early days, went to great lengths to ensure that he was able to differentiate Opus Dei from the typical Catholic denominations.

There's a story told about the first three priests who were ordained by Opus Dei. The three men – all Spanish priests – were chosen by Escriva himself to represent the organization. The attention to detail was so great that Escriva noticed that not a single man out of the three smoked cigarettes. In Spain at the time, smoking was commonplace. The fact that none of the three priests smoked made Escriva concerned. What if people believed that the priests didn't smoke due to their membership in Opus Dei? People might believe that not smoking was a part of the belief system, something that was not true. After some discussion, it was decided that one of the three men would take up smoking so as to pacify any concerns the general public might have had. It was not that Opus Dei were anti or pro cigarettes, more that it was concerned with reaching as many people as possible. The man chosen to smoke was Alvaro del Portillo, the man who would later take on Escriva's role as the head of the organization.

In a similar vein, it was decided that the priests would forgo the traditional Catholic attire, dressing instead in simpler clothes. They would not be cloistered, meaning that groups of priests would not live solitary, excluded lifestyles. Perhaps most importantly, all of the priests in Opus Dei would not claim that it had some special, sanctimonious state of life. That is to say, they were no more predisposed to sainthood than anyone else, regardless of their occupation. Rather than removing themselves from the world, these priests hoped to "Christianize" everything, hoping that their spiritual actions would set a precedent for other people to follow.

This approach was certainly revolutionary for its time. In Spain in the 1930s and 1940s, when Escriva was developing the foundations of Opus Dei, the traditional model of the Catholic Church would be considered a clergy-orientated organization. This means that the clergy would be religious leaders, elevated above the people in terms of their sanctity. For Escriva, this seemed wrong. Instead, Opus Dei focused on a model in which the clergy were on equal footing in all regards. Rather than leading people through religion, the priests were designed to act in a more supporting role. They were experts who could provide guidance and direction, rather than leaders who would strut at the head of the pack. Once the priests provided the laypeople with an understanding of God, it was down to the individual to decide how their particular actions could be made into an offering to the Lord.

In principle, this idea would suggest that Opus Dei is an organization focused on equality. As we will see later in this book, the balance between men and women in the Opus Dei has faced much criticism. In theory, female Opus Dei members receive the same spiritual coaching and direction as their male counterparts, and they are equally capable of achieving sainthood through their actions. But in many of the smaller details, the Opus Dei attitude towards women is far from an equilateral balance. At the time, however, this attitude towards equality was a marked change from the mainstream. For many centuries, the Catholic Church has had a major issue with gender equality. Even this small doctrinal change by Escriva was a step towards equality, even if the ensuing decades have revealed inherent issues with gender that were not apparent at the time.

Such breaks from the mainstream Catholic doctrine led to many people criticizing Escriva. In certain parts of Spanish society, he was denounced as being anti-clerical. Some went as far as to call him a heretic. Rumors began to circulate that he would be reported to the Vatican, the spiritual center of the Catholic world, presumably in the belief that he would be apprehended, punished, and likely excommunicated. Even in its early days, Opus Dei was controversial.

For most people, trying to come to terms with Opus Dei as an organization can be difficult. It is unlike almost every other branch of Christianity, and this seems to be intentional. Escriva himself described Opus Dei as "a disorganized organization." The people in the group are united by their shared interpretation of Catholicism and their belief in sanctifying the world from within. There is a frequently repeated phrase that gives an insight into the decentralized nature of the group: "Opus Dei doesn't act; its members do."

But is this true? Long-time critics of Opus Dei have suggested that this pretense of decentralized, independent members is a myth. Instead, Opus Dei does indeed have an intention, an organization, and a set of goals, all of which are hidden behind the smokescreen of general theology. While the majority of members might ascribe to Escriva's original vision, others are focused on seizing power, gaining financial wealth, or recruiting new members. All of these actions are kept hidden away from the public, who seem happy to believe that Opus Dei is just a particularly dedicated sect of the Catholic Church. With both sides of the argument adamant about its version of the truth, it might help to learn more about the individual requirements of each and every member. In the next chapter, we will look at what it takes to become a fully paid-up member of Opus Dei.

Joining Opus Dei

The rising profile of Opus Dei has led to a surge in the number of people who have simply walked in off the street and asked to join. A far cry from the organization's humble roots, these walk-ins have become a new phenomenon that the group has had to deal with. For a long time, the less publicized nature of Opus Dei meant that there were fewer people who even knew about them, let alone thought about joining. But is becoming a member as easy as simply strolling into your local office?

If you did decide to walk into an Opus Dei office one day and declare your intention to become a member, the first thing people would tell you is that education is important. To become a member, you should first discover more about the church's true message. However, the general path to membership does not follow this pattern. Perhaps unlike most religions, the idea of converting is not that familiar. Typically, people become members through association. This might be through a friend or a family member who is already part of Opus Dei, or through being exposed to one of the more "corporate" works, which can include schools and youth centers set up by the organization. Though there are certainly those who declare their intentions to join the group seemingly out of the blue, the majority of people are recruited through a process of friendship and association.

Once this bond is formed, then there is a gradual process of exposure. If a person has hinted to an Opus Dei member that they might be interested in joining, then they will be invited to attend meetings, either evening gatherings or retreats. At these events, the person will gain an insight into the day-to-day reality of the religion, learning how it fits into members' lives. Within the church, the code name for a recruit official joining is "whistle." When a person decides to "whistle," the moment is treated with the utmost seriousness. Opus Dei considers itself neither a hobby nor a pastime. It demands serious commitment from members, so the decision to "whistle" is regarded as a life-changing moment.

But if this decision is so important, where is the appeal for the everyday person? What could prompt a layperson to make such a massive decision? It might seem overtly simple to say that the call is a religious one. There are those who say that God pushed them in a certain, specific direction. However, there are often other factors at play. For some people, the writings that Escriva left behind have provided an inspiration. Certainly, those who have been initially interested in the church admit to having their curiosity consecrated when reading his ideas and theories about religion and work. Similarly, there is a notion that Opus Dei is able to offer a strain of religion that is both serious and supportive of the devout Catholic approach to life. Witnessing fist hand the devotion of the members, traditional Catholics might be convinced of the organization's authenticity.

Opus Dei differs from traditional religious orders in that there are no vows to be taken upon joining, as you might expect when becoming a monk or nun. Under Church law, a member's status remains exactly as it was before. Instead, Opus Dei solidifies membership using a more secular means. When joining, recruits are asked to sign a contract, entering into an agreement. The agreement states that the person will agree to live their lives in the spirit of Opus Dei, supporting the activities and doctrine that the organization sets out. In return, Opus Dei will provide spiritual formation and guidance in the way of God.

Though the contracts differ from country to country and from language to language, they are arranged in a basic formula. First, the person will announce that they are operating under their own free will and that they will, from this point onwards, dedicate themselves to the pursuit of sanctity at all times. They also pledge to "practice apostolate" in accordance with the "spirit and praxis of Opus Dei." Then, they submit to remaining under the jurisdiction of Opus Dei and dedicate themselves faithfully to the "special purposes" of the organization. Agreeing to all of Opus Dei's traditions and laws, the person finishes the contract by offering to serve under the Prelature (the local administrative branch) at all times.

In turn, the Church will offer their own contract. In return for the above dedication, the representative of the Prelate will promise to fulfil a number of obligations on the part of Opus Dei. There is a promise to "devote constant care and attention" to spiritual, doctrinal, and other religious needs. Then, there is a promise to "fulfil Opus Dei's obligations to its faithful;" that is to say, a promise to assist other members of the church in addition to this single signee.

The use of the contract is an indicator of the unique relationship between Opus Dei and its members. It's been seen as a dubious practice by those who are critical of Opus Dei, and in truth, it certainly differentiates them from the other organizations within the Catholic Church. In theory, the contract has little legal value. It does not permit, for example, members to be representatives of Opus Dei in their day-to-day lives, nor does it attempt to have any influence or control beyond spiritual guidance. But that has not stopped the speculation.

The contract has received a lot of attention from critics, but at least some of the critical speculation can be dismissed out of hand. In some of the more conspiratorial corners of the internet, discussions about contracts signed in blood and the selling of the soul have been linked with Opus Dei. Of all the contracts that have been made public – and there is no clause or tradition preventing them from being revealed – neither of these factors have been present. They are simply part of the urban legend commonly associated with Opus Dei.

But other critics often point towards the possibility that the "spiritual guidance" that Opus Dei promises to provide can be corrupting. If, for example, a member was in a particularly high-powered position, people have pointed at the clauses within the contract and suggesting that the organization might attempt to influence a person's work for the benefit of Opus Dei. This might be closing a big business deal or enacting a piece of legislature, either of which could either be profitable for Opus Dei or could ratify elements of their ideology. Opus Dei's contract, the critics say, provides them with the power to intervene and influence members in a professional capacity. The Work of God, as suggested within the contract, is one and the same as the work of the individual.

There is little evidence to support this claim, however. Indeed, those members of the church whom we know to have held powerful positions have not only dismissed the suggestion, but have declared that the opposite is true. Luis Valls, for example, was both the chairman of Spain's third largest commercial bank and a member of Opus Dei. In charge of a company worth almost $50 billion, he says he was never told what to do by anyone within the organization. In fact, he claims, the spiritual guidance of Opus Dei helped to keep him on the right moral track. Without Opus Dei, Valls says, he would have been a "rascal."

While it might not seem to be too controversial, this element of the Opus Dei operation can be one of the most criticized. The recruitment of new members is something that is often little understood and has caused a great deal of speculation in many circles. How does the group pick is targets? Are they too pushy and intimidating in their recruitment? What is their long-term goal? We will examine some of these accusations in a later chapter, but some people have made the claim that Opus Dei resembles a cult. As we continue with our basic overview of the organization, this can be something that is worth keeping in mind, before we directly address the issue later.

First, we should look at the idea of "whistling." In its purest sense, whistling refers to the act of writing a letter, asking to join Opus Dei. It's a formal process, known in documentation as "requesting admission." The term "whistling," however, was used by Escriva himself, in reference to the whistling sound made by steam escaping from a boiling kettle. Just as the water had reached a boiling point and is ready to pour, the prospective member has reached their own point of readiness. Age doesn't really matter. Whistling is possible from the ages of sixteen and a half upwards. However, there is a requirement that an individual must be eighteen years old before they can formally be incorporated into the church. Indeed, from fourteen and a half years old, it is possible to register as an "aspirant," in preparation for more formal inclusion at an older age. Whistling is not guaranteed to work. It's not uncommon for prospective members to write a number of letters before Opus Dei deems them ready to continue with their formal application.

The next step is admission. Once the formal application has been approved, there is a short ceremony for members. The process involves two members of Opus Dei, typically a priest and a lay director. These two people will listen to the prospective member's verbal pledge to live their life "in the spirit" of Opus Dei, who in turn will promise to provide means of spiritual formation. This ceremony typically occurs six months after the whistling, during which time the person has lived their life as an informal Opus Dei member, following the ideas of the organization and being treated as a member.

Once admission is complete, a person will move on to "oblation." This usually takes place eighteen months after a person has whistled, and it marks the signing of the contract between an individual and Opus Dei. This commitment is set for annual renewal, usually on the 19th of March. The date is important in the Catholic Church as it is the Feast of St. Joseph, who is said to be the patron saint of workers and Opus Dei alike. The oblation is not considered a permanent agreement, though those who choose to break it and turn away from

Opus Dei are treated seriously. Within the church, this is a "grave matter," a seemingly purposefully broad statement. The oblation is done privately in tandem with personal prayer. Once a member has renewed their agreement, they are required to tell the organization. If they do not, then they are automatically disavowed and are no longer considered a member.

Being a member of Opus Dei is an ongoing commitment. Unlike many other churches in which one might be able to dip in and out as it pleases, there is a need for constant reapplication to the organization. One such commitment is the "fidelity," which takes places five years after the completion of the first oblation. It's a lifetime commitment to Opus Dei, though it only needs to be made once. As soon as it is complete, then the person is considered to be a permanent member of Opus Dei, part of the "supernatural family." After this point, leaving the organization becomes more difficult. Departing members are required to write a formal letter, though those who are more desperate to leave have been known to skip this step. Due to the age restrictions on whistling and oblation, the minimum age for the fidelity is 23, though there is no upper limit on age.

Once you have become a member, you will join the ranks of some 85,000 Opus Dei practitioners worldwide. These are the numbers kept by the Vatican itself, which keeps track of the involvement of people within the organization. Of the 85,000, just under 2,000 are priests. The ratio of priests to clergy is close to roughly 45:1. But within the main body of the laity, the membership can be broken down even further. The distinctions between the categories of members in Opus Dei are usually arranged by the organization in terms of how available a certain person is for church activities. Typical distinctions based on careers, employment, or "grades" of devoutness and holiness are not present. Instead, the categories are:

1. Supernumeraries and numeraries, and another subset, numerary assistants
2. Associates
3. Cooperators (who are not members, but do support Opus Dei.)

It's terms such as these that have often given people cause to compare Opus Dei to a secret society. The idea of structured membership is something that is present in groups such as the Freemasons, especially as the names for the categories are not familiar to most. In fact, they are taken from Opus Dei's Spanish background, being the nomenclature used for the types of professor at a university. It's somewhat ironic that a stylistic choice that was meant to make Opus Dei more relatable and ordinary has, in the 21st Century, had the opposite effect.

Let's take a look at the individual categories, starting with the **supernumeraries**. This is the category that includes roughly 70% of Opus Dei members. Due to the way in which categorization works, these are the individuals whom the church considers least available. Whether it's family commitments or the like, supernumeraries have distinctly less time to dedicate to the church. Because of this, they live in their homes, just like a regular person might. In a marriage, it's possible for both partners to be supernumeraries or just one. For supernumeraries, spiritual direction is received from an Opus Dei numerary – typically the director of the local center – and confession is conducted by an Opus Dei priest.

In terms of public attention, the supernumeraries are perhaps the unheralded majority of Opus Dei. While they are overwhelmingly in the majority, the focus usually sways to the numeraries or the priests. There are some, however, who claim that it is the supernumeraries who are the real force within the church. In terms of Opus Dei's objective of transforming the way we live our everyday lives, the supernumeraries represent that policy in action. The sheer number of supernumeraries is closer to the church's long-term objectives like setting up a charity school.

Part of the responsibility of the supernumeraries is the financial contributions they are expected to make to Opus Dei. These are handled on a personal basis. While the well-off might make large contributions, those who are less financially privileged will not be expected to match their contributions. These are handled on a "pay what you can afford" type of arrangement. It's something of a misconception that the majority of Opus Dei members are upper-middle class, white collar workers. While this might be true for many members, the organization spans far more of the social spectrum than might be expected. This is what helps contribute to the idea of the "hidden majority" that some have used to criticize Opus Dei.

In addition to being members of Opus Dei, it is not uncommon for supernumeraries to continue to hold a place in other religious organizations. They remain active in their local parishes and dioceses, with many actively contributing to the community as members of the parish council, as lectors, leaders of youth groups, and many other positions. Opus Dei, for these individuals, is not an exclusive commitment and can function in tandem with previous involvement in church organizations. However, if the supernumeraries are the presentable face of the Opus Dei membership, then it is the numeraries themselves who attract the vast majority of the attention from the outside world.

The **numeraries** form roughly 20% of the Opus Dei membership. Chiefly, they are comprised of members who have dedicated themselves to the Opus Dei family. To be one of the numeraries, one must make a series of pledges. These include commitments of celibacy, and in some cases, giving up a career to work full time for Opus Dei. For the majority of numeraries, however, a position outside of the church is common, though professions typically involve some degree of professional expertise. This means that many are surgeons, lawyers, writers, or similarly focused careerists. From these professions, any money that is not required to live is passed to the coffers of Opus Dei and used for church activities. For many American numeraries, this has led to issues with the IRS, in which the taxmen find it incomprehensible that people could make such large charitable donations, sometimes as much as three-quarters of a yearly salary.

Numeraries are known to enjoy a more rigorous, extensive education in religious, spiritual, and theological matters. Because of this, they are often entrusted with a greater number of leadership positions within the church. In the case of an Opus Dei center, for example, only a numerary is permitted to take on the role of director. Sometimes, this education extends to sending numeraries to Rome, so that they will be able to study theology in a formal setting, often at the famous University of the Holy Cross.

Of all the numeraries, there is an even smaller subset who are known as the "inscripti." These Opus Dei members are trusted enough to offer doctrinal and spiritual formation to other church members. They play a notable part in the importance of the numeraries and Opus Dei in general. When the organization is hoping to expand into a new area, a certain number of numeraries and inscripti are required in order to lay the foundations for the new center. The geographical expansion of Opus Dei depends upon these dedicated members in order to maintain a certain level of religious and spiritual commitment and consistency.

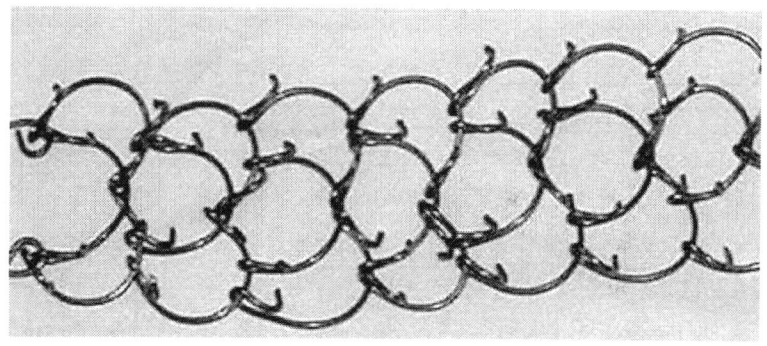

But the numeraries are also important in that it is often their practices that draw the attention of those most critical of Opus Dei. As we will see later in this book, a number of their most controversial practices involved self-flagellation and corporal discipline. The "cilice," for example, is a small chain fitted with rows of metal spikes. It is fastened on the upper thigh of the numeraries for a few hours each day (excluding Sundays and feast days). The spikes dig into the flesh and cause the wearer pain. In addition to the cilice, there is the "discipline." The discipline is the name for the short whip, used once a week during prayer time. The user whips the cord-like device across their back during the Our Father, again causing pain.

Becoming a numerary is a demanding position. It not only requires a great deal of spiritual and financial commitment, but the self-punishment aspect of the practice stands out among almost all Christian denominations. It's this pain-inducing mode of worship that draws the attention of outsiders, but as we will soon discover, it is done with a certain religious purpose. It's a demonstration of the commitment demanded of the numeraries by Opus Dei and makes many people distrustful of their activities. However, the numeraries do not work alone.

The **numerary assistants** are another subset of the Opus Dei membership structure. Numbering close to 4,000 and all of them women, the numerary assistants are another seemingly-strange branch of the Opus Dei membership. These women are known for their full-time devotion to the running of the Opus Dei centers and the other facilities that are owned and operated by the Organization. While the numeraries might live in an Opus Dei center while working a full-time job, the numerary assistants will remain within the center and handle chores such as cooking or cleaning, as well as the financial management of the center. The position has been likened to that of a full-time mother, which is often the way the numerary assistants themselves see the position.

The idea for this position has often been attributed to Escriva's own family life. The founder wanted all Opus Dei centers to have the feeling of a home rather than an organization. In order to accomplish this, he decided that they would require "a woman's touch." The women who fill these positions are paid for their work, which is regarded by Opus Dei as a full-time position. When carrying out the work around the center, numerary assistants typically have a uniform that signifies their position. While cooking or cleaning in an Opus Dei center, it's possible to recognize the numerary assistants purely through their choice of clothing.

But this is yet another position that has drawn negative attention to Opus Dei. The role and the requirements of the numerary assistants has been described as outdated and sexist, suggestive of a regressive view of women. Opus Dei, say numerous critics, is responsible for promoting a submissive and harmfully traditionalist view of gender roles. This is not helped when, in defense of their organization, Opus Dei members have suggested that they are not discriminating by simply noting women's skills in the domestic sphere. It is a skillset that they firmly believe men lack. Added to this, the role of the numerary assistants is part of Escriva's original vision for Opus Dei and not open to debate. It's perhaps not unexpected that such a hardline, traditionalist branch of the Catholic Church should hold outdated ideas of gender roles, but it certainly becomes another stick with which critics can beat Opus Dei when required. The organization does not help themselves with responses, but these practices often seem outdated rather than suspicious in the minds of many of the more critical opponents of Opus Dei.

The **associates** are a group within Opus Dei who are similar to the numeraries. Just like the numeraries, they remain celibate, though they often have family members and personal reasons as to why they live away from

Opus Dei centers. The most important distinction to make between associates and numeraries is their living arrangements. Other than one group living in the Opus Dei centers and one group enjoying more conventional residence, they have the same spiritual expectations. They can both work in almost any position, providing they do so in a manner that complies with the organization's view on work as a tribute to God. It might be that an associate has younger brothers or sisters who depend on them being at home, or that the associate's particular career path has taken them to a part of the world without a local Opus Dei center. It's possible to move between groups, going from being a supernumerary to an associate depending on current circumstances.

An important role within the church that we have yet to mention is that of the **priests**. With just under two thousand clergy members "incardinated" into the Opus Dei organization, they are not the largest division within the Catholic Church by any means. A central authority – known as the prelate – resides in Rome and acts as the guiding figure for the Opus Dei priests. Typically, an Opus Dei priest will carry out the conventional duties of a Catholic priest, including pastoral care, running the parish affairs, and organizing Church activities. They might occasionally hold teaching positions in universities or seminaries. The vast majority of priests have been recruited from the Opus Dei numeraries and differ slightly from most Catholic priests in their relationship to the Church members. Whereas traditionally, priests might be spiritual superiors and leaders, Opus Dei's clergy function in more of a support role.

The priests are assisted by a group known as the **cooperators**. Though not technically Opus Dei members, the cooperators are "friends" of the organization and will often offer their support in a number of ways. This might be through prayer, through organizational assistance, or even through financial donations. The cooperators do not have to be Catholic or even Christian. In a move that has raised more than a few cynical eyebrows, Opus Dei's cooperators are often Jewish, Muslim, Buddhist, or non-theists. As a matter of fact, Opus Dei became the first Catholic organization that had the right to enroll people who were not actually Catholics, a law passed in 1950. This has caused criticism from people within the Catholic Church, especially traditionalists. The claim is that such a move makes Opus Dei appear as "indifferentist" (that all religions are of equal validity) and that the order fails to recognize Catholicism as being the foremost among many religions.

However, this has done nothing to dent the number of cooperators whom Opus Dei count around the world. At last count, this number was as high as 164,000, of whom almost 60% are women. Furthermore, there are as many as 900,000 people who are part of an even wider network and involved with Opus Dei, taking part in events and activities, perhaps laying the foundations for eventually being considered as official cooperators. These people swell the ranks of the Opus Dei membership considerably, though it is not only individuals who are counted.

As well as people, Opus Dei has registered almost 500 separate religious communities who are counted as cooperators. These can be men and women, such as communities of monks or nuns, who have formed good working relationships with Opus Dei centers, even if they do not share exactly the same beliefs. A shared spiritual background and a shared effort in building strong bonds with local religious groups means that many Opus Dei centers have fostered cooperative relationships with people and groups in their area. All of this helps with the spreading of the organization's message.

With many diverse roles within Opus Dei and many different people enjoying dissimilar levels of commitment, trying to pin down exact paths to joining the organization can be difficult. Part of this mystery is why so many find the group to be intriguing and different. While most churches will accept anyone through their doors, Opus Dei's recruitment is markedly different from not only the majority of the Catholic Church, but other religions as well. But this has not held them back. In the next chapter, we will take a look at how the group has spread across the world, as well as a closer look at the man responsible.

A Global Concern

Despite its relatively low membership numbers compared to many other religious organizations, Opus Dei has become a global enterprise. Though its base remains largely in Europe, its growth and expansion has been somewhat remarkable for an organization founded less than a hundred years ago. But where do the majority of their members reside?

Perhaps unsurprisingly, the country with by far the most Opus Dei members is Spain. The founder of the organization, Escriva, was a Spanish priest whose once tiny organization has turned into a 35,000 strong group in his home country, mostly in Madrid. This amounts to roughly 40% of the global membership figures. Though Opus Dei was founded in the earliest decades of the 20th Century, initial plans for expansion were hampered by the political situation in Spain. The outbreak of the Spanish Civil War in the 1930s, for example, led to utter turmoil in the country and sank many of Escriva's initial plans.

By the 1940s, plans for expansion were set into motion. In 1946, for example, Opus Dei moved into Italy, Portugal, and Great Britain, three of the traditionally most important countries in Europe. This was followed a year later by moves into France and Ireland. In 1949, Opus Dei began to cross the Atlantic Ocean, and centers opened in the USA, Mexico, Chile, Argentina, Colombia, and Venezuela. Throughout the 1950s, the organization continued to expand in Europe and the Americas, moving into Germany, Guatemala, Peru, Ecuador, Uruguay, Switzerland, Brazil, Austria, and

Canada. By 1959, the first steps were made into Asia and Africa, with centers opening in Japan and Kenya, as well as El Salvador, Costa Rica, and Holland.

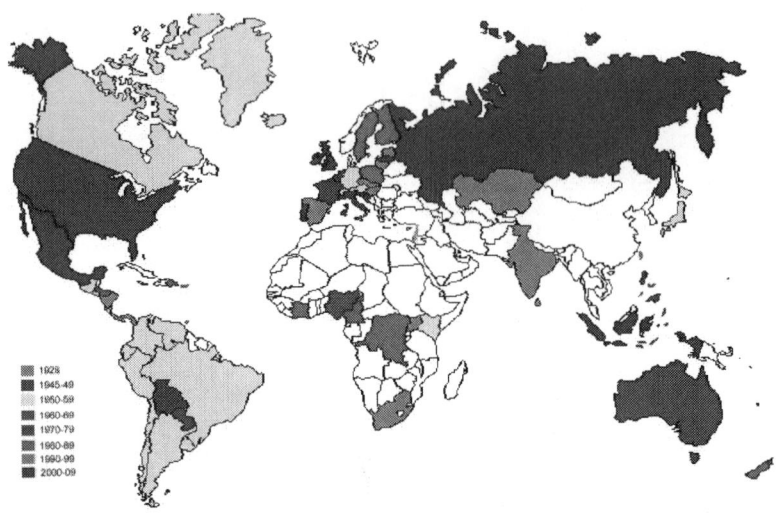

Through the 1960s, Opus Dei expanded into Paraguay, Australia, the Philippines, Belgium, Nigeria, and Puerto Rico, meaning it had a base of operation on almost every continent. This expansion slowed in the 1970s, with only Bolivia being added to the list, though the 1980s saw the Ivory Coast, the Congo, Honduras, Hong Kong, Singapore, Trinidad, Tobago, Sweden, Taiwan, Finland, Cameroon, the Dominican Republic, Macao, New Zealand and Poland added to the list. It was a pattern continued through the 1990s, a time in which Hungary, the Czech Republic, Nicaragua, India, Israel, Lithuania, Estonia, Slovakia, Lebanon, Panama, Uganda, Kazakhstan, and South Africa all became countries hosting Opus Dei centers. In recent years, Slovenia, Croatia, and Lithuania have welcomed Opus Dei. As you can see, over the past seventy years, the rate of expansion has been impressive.

Despite the wide-ranging nature of the above list of countries, it is no surprise to see that the bulk of the membership numbers for Opus Dei comes from countries that have a longstanding relationship with Catholicism. The list of countries that boast the most Opus Dei members are (in order):

1. Spain
2. Mexico
3. Argentina
4. Italy
5. The United States of America
6. The Philippines
7. Colombia

As you can see, the top three are all Spanish-speaking countries, followed by Italy (home of the Vatican) and the United States (one of the world's most populous countries). There are a number of countries that one might expect to see on the list, but for one reason or another, they have not embraced Opus Dei to the same extent.

The United Kingdom was one of the first places Escriva visited when trying to expand Opus Dei. Indeed, London was one of his favorite cities, and he was heard to refer to it as a "crossroads of the world." Escriva even had favorite museums and churches in the city, in particular the Anglican Church of St. Duncan. The church held the tomb of the Roper family and was the final resting place for the head of St. Thomas More, one of Escriva's heroes. But despite this love of the country and almost six decades spent in Great Britain, Opus Dei has barely more than five hundred British members. On average, they're able to recruit fewer than ten each year. Part of the reason for this might be the work of Cardinal Basil Hume, a priest who warned about the dangers of Opus Dei in a particularly public manner. As Hume's words reached other bishops, and in turn, the Catholics of Britain, the name of Opus Dei was tarnished before they could establish a particularly strong foothold.

It's worth comparing the relative failure in Britain to Opus Dei's success in countries like Peru. In this South American country, the popularity of Opus Dei and of Escriva in particular is slightly astonishing. Despite its small size and its unimportance in geopolitical terms, Peru accounts for close to 2% of Opus Dei's global membership, almost three times that of Britain. Among these 1,600 people are 400 numeraries and just under 200 associates. There are also 200 priests, 11 active bishops, and even 2 Peruvian Opus Dei bishops who work overseas. This, in particular, is amazing, considering that Peru's Opus Dei bishops amount to roughly a third of the global total.

Peru represents what can happen when the power of Opus Dei is allowed to flourish inside a country. Rather than traditional Catholicism, it's easy to note the prevalence of Opus Dei's influence in the region of Canete. The organization was given a Papal prelature in 1957, allowing Opus Dei to invest the Vatican's money in establishing Church infrastructure in the country. The lasting legacy of this is not only that Opus Dei is overly represented when compared to other countries, but that Escriva's name is held in high reverence throughout Peru.

But now that we know about the global reach of Opus Dei, one question remains on many people's lips. What exactly do Opus Dei members do? In order to earn their reputation as one of the most controversial religious bodies in the world, mustn't their activities garner some attention from the outside world? Again, this is difficult to ascertain. Thus far, we have avoided stepping too far into the controversial secrets of Opus Dei. So far, we have examined the skeletal structure of the Church, taking only a few pauses here and there to note the more controversial elements. This provides us with a firm understanding of the church, so that we will better be able to explore the divisive elements in a later chapter. In much the same way, in order to learn about why Opus Dei remains controversial, we must learn about their activities and what it is that they do on a day-by-day basis.

Whenever you ask Opus Dei members what it is that they "do," you're likely to receive a stock answer. We're already covered the unique nature of Opus Dei's approach to work, in that everything they do should somehow be directed towards sanctification and God. Accordingly, it's not a surprise to hear answers such as work, family, church events, and other general, everyday activities. The only difference is that the members use even non-religious activities to line their path towards holiness. So while even the most mundane answer to the question "what do Opus Dei members do," might seem bland and uninteresting, every single response is imbued with the particular theology of the organization. That is to say, Opus Dei members might appear as though they are carrying out typical tasks, but the manner in which they approach said tasks is very different when compared to non-members.

However, while church members might view every activity as part of a greater goal, there are some traditions, rituals, and processes that are taught by the Opus Dei leadership and carried out by most members. Through the course of a typical day, these might be used a number of times.

For example, for many Opus Dei members, the day begins with an offering. The day itself is offered to God in a short prayer, repeating the phrase "I will serve" as an indication of how the day's work will be dedicated to God. After this, members might partake in a daily mass, receiving communion in the traditional Catholic fashion, and then having a praying of the rosary. Following this, many members set aside thirty minutes during both the morning and the evening to have a personal, mental prayer. At noon, this is joined by an Angelus prayer or the Regina Coeli, depending on the time of the year. Every day, members look inwards and examine their own conscience. There is a meditation lasting roughly ten minutes, during which time the individual will consider the recent spiritual teachings they have received, as well as dedicating five minutes of each day to hearing a reading from the New Testament.

Opus Dei members usually pay a daily visit to the Blessed Sacrament, usually following the last meal of the day. This often involves the saying of Our Father's, Hail Mary's, and Glory Be's, all of which are prayers to make up a "spiritual communion." This is the Opus Dei term for any union with Jesus Christ that does not involve the taking of the daily communion. As well as this, there is a set of prayers that are all in Latin. These are named the Preces, and they are said each day, invocating Jesus, Mary, the Holy Spirit, Saint Joseph,

Saint José Maria, the Guardian Angels, as well as more conventional prayers for the Pope, the local bishops, anyone who is working to spread the gospel, Opus Dei's prelate, Opus Dei members, and anyone else who might be deserving. Following this, there are invocations to a number of Saints, such as John, Peter, Paul, Gabriel, Raphael, and Michael.

As you can see, the amount of reflection, prayer time, dedication, and tradition is above and beyond what is expected of most religious people. As Opus Dei members believe that all of their working lives are part of their religious offering, it can be surprising to see the amount of prayer and conventional religious activity that is also required. But these are not the only practices done by Opus Dei members. As well as the above, there are also those who carry out more specific acts.

"Aspirations" is the name given to the short prayers that are said at regular intervals throughout the day. These might be something like "Jesus, Mary, and Joseph, I give you my heart and soul," or "Jesus, I love you with all of my heart." Many of the wordings are handed down from the prelate of Opus Dei, including a recent one that said "Everything with Peter to Jesus through Mary." Similarly, some members use holy water in order to purify themselves before going to bed for the night. This can be combined with a number of Hail Mary's. Furthermore, the corporal mortification that we have already alluded to is just another example of the kind of Opus Dei religious dedication that really sets them apart from other organizations.

In addition to the everyday activities that the church encourages, Opus Dei organize regular events designed to help with members' religiosity. This includes the "circle," a class delivered by a layperson that focuses on some theological element of Opus Dei, as well as containing a section that helps members examine their conscience. This works in tandem with monthly recollection meetings, which are made up of a few meditation sessions and delivered by a priest. Once a year, supernumeraries attend Opus Dei workshops. These can last several days, while numeraries typically have an annual course that they can attend. Furthermore, there are often Opus Dei retreats that can provide several days' worth of religious education and affirmation crammed into a short period. Sometimes, these retreats can be conducted almost entirely in silence, encouraging deeper stages of meditation. While these events are happening, members will continue to receive spiritual guidance from associates and numeraries.

In order to learn about these practices, members will often receive a document titled Catechism of Opus Dei. Now up to at least its seventh edition, the document is roughly 130 pages long and is not distributed to the general public. It is designed for internal use only, often being used to guide prayer, meditation, and reflection meetings. It's organized in a question-and-answer format, designed to provide solutions to the issues faced by members. The document has been published for many years and not without controversy. Escriva himself had to write a short note in a previous edition explaining why it was being withdrawn from circulation, citing the "intense and hidden opposition to the Work" as the reason. The passage does not go into depth on the exact nature of this opposition, but it was enough for the church leaders to believe that the Catechism of Opus Dei might be dangerous if it fell into the wrong hands. The modern edition of the document contains a history of Opus Dei and a number of deliberations on theological matters. If there was indeed controversial information being distributed to members, it has since been removed.

For the numeraries of Opus Dei, life inside the center is even more regimented. For example, they are required to attend a daily meeting known as the "tertulia," which has been likened to a family get together for those who live in the building. Here, they will receive an education akin to the seminary studies that a trainee priest might receive. The yearly retreats for numeraries are often longer, sometimes taking as long as three weeks, such is the intensity of the course. Added to their religious devotions, numeraries are expected to make themselves available for Opus Dei-related activities. This might be helping out in a youth center or organizing church-related events. It might be helping to tackle unforeseen problems around the center or helping with visitors and newer members. These kinds of tasks are considered family activities and, again, are carried out with the same degree of sanctimony and religious forethought.

At the same time as these smaller rituals, practices, and traditions are being exercised, it is expected that all members of Opus Dei will have some kind of employment. This is not a unilateral requirement, in that the type of employment can vary on a case by case basis. When asking what it is that Opus Dei does, work is an essential part of their belief system. That means that the job might be a banker or a homemaker, but each role is approached with a spiritual element. But in addition to this, there is the work that members are expected to carry out on behalf of the church. This could involve helping at the Opus Dei center or even serving at the national or international headquarters. Whatever it is that they are doing, there is an expectation from Opus Dei that all members will strive to work as hard as possible and to achieve the highest standards available in every capacity of their working lives.

Though these expectations might appear taxing to those who do not involve religion in their lives to any great extent, Opus Dei members are often left with some time free to themselves. At this point, they are essentially allowed to do what they please. At least, in an official capacity, Opus Dei members are allowed to spend their free time in any way they please, so long as they apply the same devotional religious ideas to anything they might try to accomplish. In fact, the Opus Dei doctrine is applied in almost every area of life. Members are asked to consider the religious ramifications of their careers, their friendships, their political decisions, their hobbies, even the choices they make as a consumer. All activity should be carried out with the Opus Dei doctrine in mind. While the church might not tell people exactly what to do – who to vote for or what brands to buy, for example – they will ask members to think about spiritual matters in every facet of their lives. In that respect, everything an Opus Dei member does is somehow colored by their religion.

Part of the devotional practice of Opus Dei's doctrine includes work done for the church. These projects can include youth centers, schools, agricultural endeavors, and many other types of work. Often, taking part in one of these projects will be accompanied by a doctrinal message on how this work relates to the church and to God. In all, Opus Dei members have worked on a huge number of projects around the world. These have included:

- The running of 15 universities for the benefit of 80,000 students. Perhaps the most famous is the University of Navarra, located in Pamplona, Spain, which allows students to study law, philosophy, medicine, theology, economics, communications, and many other subjects. In addition, campuses in Rome and Guatemala show that these educational facilities are a global concern.
- There are seven Opus Dei hospitals, institutions that employ over a thousand doctors and fifteen hundred nurses. At any one time, they could be treating as many as 300,000 patients. Locations include Congo and Nigeria, providing health care in less-equipped regions.
- Opus Dei runs eleven business schools with as many as ten thousand students in locations such as Mexico, Barcelona, and Buenos Aires.
- There are more than 35 primary and secondary schools run by Opus Dei around the world, five of which are in the USA. Others are in places such as Kenya and Japan.
- Opus Dei has nearly 100 technical schools teaching vocational skills, often located purposefully in poorer neighborhoods. These can teach English and Spanish as second languages to children, teenagers, and adults in countries such as Italy, Brazil, the Philippines, Peru, and Guatemala.

- Opus Dei provides residences to 6,000 students in at least 165 locations around the world, the majority of whom are not members of the organization. These living quarters will often include libraries, study areas, and academic assistance, as well as offering spiritual and religious guidance. These are located in Holland, Spain, Taiwan, and London.

As well as these Opus Dei-related institutions, there are others that are not run by the organization, but rather are affiliated with them. That means that two universities, a business school, 213 primary and secondary schools, 59 vocational colleges, an untold number of medical clinics, and 27 pharmacies have all received assistance in some form or another from Opus Dei in recent years. The group is happy to discuss their involvement in such matters, especially considering that many of these projects provide good PR for a much-maligned organization. In addition, they provide many Opus Dei members with potential volunteer work if and when they have the time to spare. In addition to those projects listed above, it is not uncommon for members to devise and implement their own ideas for charitable efforts in the community. These might be subject to Opus Dei's approval and might receive backing from the group, though are rarely mentioned in official documentation. Despite this, many of these projects will somehow adhere to the organization's theological principles.

The difference between the official and unofficial works in regards to Opus Dei is significant. The former, commonly called "corporate works," are those that have an official relation to the organization. Trying to differentiate between these and the works that are simply carried out by members is something that has troubled outside observers for a long time. Both are staffed with Opus Dei members and carried out in the spirit of the organization, so why the difference? Some have suggested that tax liabilities in certain countries might be the reason, though Opus Dei denies this. Instead, the official reasoning is three fold. First, it might be that unofficial works are carried out by non-Catholics. Second, Opus Dei has said that it does not want to stifle members' creative instincts by providing too many suggestions. Finally, it is said that there might be the possibility that the secularity of Opus Dei's works would be compromised. Despite affiliation with the church, Opus Dei hopes that its agents and members will be viewed as individuals, rather than people working on the organization's behalf. Escriva himself once announced his disgust at those who attempted to use their Catholicism to attain special privileges, so Opus Dei attempts to make this a non-issue. In doing so, however, they muddy the waters between personal and official Opus Dei projects, something that can make trying to keep track of the organization's activities slightly more difficult.

However, everything we have seen thus far has very much been in the public view. It's not uncommon for large religious organizations to be involved in charitable ventures, nor is it uncommon that they would involve their members in such endeavors. But once you start looking closely at the inner workings of Opus Dei (especially in relation to the Vatican), then the picture begins to look very different. Firstly, we should examine what is known as the personal prelature.

Perhaps the first encounter with the controversial side of Opus Dei in the English-speaking world occurred in 1982. At the time, the media's attention was not focused in any way on the organization. Some people might have known them as a particularly devout denomination within the Catholic Church, but there was little attention paid to either Opus Dei or their activities. This changed when Opus Dei was granted canonical status by Pope John Paul II providing the organization with a "personal prelature," which is kind of like a personal, unique diocese defined by contract rather than geography. The "prelate" refers to the man – usually a bishop – who is chosen to run the prelature. It's a strange part of the Catholic legislature but one with important ramifications.

What it meant was that Opus Dei members were distinct within the Catholic Church. On the normal matters of Catholicism, they would defer to their local Catholic priest, whether they were in Nairobi, Rome, or Tokyo. So for example, processes such as obtaining a marriage annulment would proceed through the normal channels of Catholicism. But it amounted to a formal recognition of Opus Dei's rules and doctrines. Furthermore, it was a kind of permission from the Catholic Church for Opus Dei members to be subject to the prelature and its rules in parts of their lives that were not normally governed by the Church. In other words, it put an official stamp on the pervasive and somewhat controlling grip in which Opus Dei holds its members. But that's not the only reason the prelature was controversial. To this date, the personal prelature granted to Opus Dei remains unique. No other organization in the world enjoys such a privilege.

The history of the personal prelature can be traced back to the Second Vatican Council, which took place in 1965. This was a massive examination and modernization of exactly how the Catholic Church was organized, and the establishment of the personal prelature was made possible during this time. By 1983, the Vatican had published a new Code of Canon Law, a set of rules for Catholicism that included Opus Dei as the one and only personal prelature in the world. The move sent shock waves through the religious community and was soon picked up by the wide world. People began to open their eyes to Opus Dei and began to question just why this small branch of the Church was being given such privileged positions.

For most people, the reason for Opus Dei's favored status seemed to be linked to their founder. Escriva had been trained as a lawyer, though his graduating thesis at the seminary had concerned an "extraordinary case of quasi-episcopal jurisdiction" as it pertained to a medieval Spanish convent. As such, Escriva was one of the world's leading scholars on the finer details of the Catholic Church's canon and judiciary. More than anyone, he knew the rules and regulations right down to the fine print. It should be no surprise that the history of Escriva's Opus Dei's organization can fill over 650 pages of legal history in the church, broadly documented in *The Canonical Path of Opus Dei: The History and Defense of a Charism*.

It was in 1941 that Escriva's organization was first approved and gained the status of a pious union. This was followed by a merger with another group, the Priestly Society of the Holy Cross, two years later. By 1947, the organization had become a secular institute, free from the official oversight of the Catholic Church. This placed Opus Dei in the perfect position for the 1982 declaration as a personal prelature. Most men would not have known how to navigate the choppy waters of the Catholic bureaucracy, but Escriva was a master.

Opus Dei members themselves, however, are keen to argue that their growth was not a quest for special privileges. Instead, they suggest that they sought to find a canonical means of protecting the original vision of their founder. To give an example of how Escriva managed to turn the Catholic codes to his advantage, take a look at the Code of Canon Law from 1917. Canon 500 of this document declares that a secular institute is not permitted to be composed of people of both genders. As such, the laws suggest that Opus Dei should have been split into two distinct bodies, one for men and one for women. By the time the personal prelature came into effect in 1983, however, this requirement was removed. Opus Dei is the only personal prelature and thus the only organization within the Catholic Church that does not have to observe this rule (or many others.)

It's this awarding of the canonical status that is difficult to underplay in the history of Opus Dei. To the outsider, it might look like boring and insipid disagreements over rules and regulations. But the Catholic Church is nearly two millennia old and these laws have been observed for centuries. It is these same laws that dictate the way in which religion is implemented to the millions of Catholics around the world. That they should allow Opus Dei to be exempt on one hand and so close to the Vatican on the other seems to indicate that the organization – despite Opus Dei's protestations – has managed to wrangle a special set of privileges for itself.

Thanks to this privileged position, Opus Dei can occupy a unique place within the Catholic Church. They are able to insist on their own singularity, they are able to maintain a standoffish attitude with regards to other religious and secular organizations, they are able to remain fussy and demanding about the vocabulary and categories of the Church's canon, and their constant quest for approval from the highest authorities within the Vatican ae much better explained. Once you realize that Opus Dei's special position within the Church grants them singular privileges, there emerges an image of an organization that is not as confident as they might otherwise appear. Opus Dei, as a personal prelature, walks a fine line and are seemingly always worried about slipping to either side. They might fall to the way of a religious order, which would distance them from the vast majority of lay people who would see them as just another church. Or they might fall too far the other way and be seen as a secular organization, which would provide no room for priests or theology. Instead, Opus Dei's concept of the priests and the lay people as being constituent parts of a greater whole is a finely balanced proposition. Importantly, it is not a part of the Catholic tradition. Rarely in the history of the Catholic Church had the ideas of Opus Dei been spoken about or adhered to. The personal prelature, then, acts as a form of protection for this finely balanced proposition. It provides Opus Dei with the traditional authority of the Catholic Church. Rather than being a bureaucratic move for power, Escriva's manipulation of the canonical regulations provided protection for a fledgling religious order. When viewed like this, Opus Dei looks much less threatening.

In the above section, a reference was made to the Priestly Society of the Holy Cross. It can help to understand this organization better, especially in terms of how it relates to Opus Dei. In simple terms, the Priestly Society of the Holy Cross is an organization that unites both the Opus Dei priests with priests from other dioceses. This association allows them to share and discuss doctrine and spirituality, especially with regards to the Opus Dei idea of formation. It's something that is written into the laws of the Catholic Church. Specifically, Canon 278 of the Code of Canon Law provides diocesan priests with the right to join up with any spiritual association they might choose. It's a form of independence for the many priests of the Catholic Church.

The matter was a personal concern for Escriva. So worried was he about the formation of the Church's priests that he came very close to actually leaving Opus Dei \ in order to found a new organization that would permit the uniting of priests as they saw fit. In the end, Escriva decided that he would be able to accomplish this goal within Opus Dei and created a society that united priests, whether they were in Opus Dei or not. Within this society, only the priests formally acknowledged as being a part of Opus Dei are bound by the prelate's jurisdiction, technically referred to as the "incardination." This means that these priests come under the direct authority of Opus Dei. Those priests who are incardinated into Opus Dei's prelature will then be considered numeraries, while those who are incardinated in their own dioceses still will be counted as either associates or supernumeraries. The distinction is typically made with regards to how much time is available to dedicate to the Opus Dei activities, but all are considered to be involved with the Opus Dei community.

It's a vision established by Escriva, who deemed that diocesan priests (that is, those who are not Opus Dei priests) would be able to sanctify their work, but in order to do so, they might develop a strong relationship with the bishop. For diocesan priests, their means of sanctifying work is to follow the word of those further up the Catholic chain of command. That's where the Priestly Society of the Holy Cross comes in. It is not designed to replace the bishop in this situation. The society does not intend to become the primary point of reference for priests. Indeed, it's even possible for bishops themselves to be members of the society. Instead, the Priestly Society of the Holy Cross hopes to promote holiness within its many members through the fulfilment of their duties as priests. Just as a carpenter might turn his work into a religious expression were he an Opus Dei member, the Society allows for priests to do the same, using their position within the Church in a different manner to the standard Opus Dei priests. While still fulfilling their duties as Catholic priests, the Society offers the men a chance to learn Opus Dei's teachings at the same time.

The society was a creation of Escriva in 1943. Partly, it was designed to ensure that priests were never in short supply for Opus Dei members. At the time, Opus Dei was not the global organization it is today, so by using Catholic by-laws and regulations to skirt around a few of the doctrinal issues, Escriva was able to swell the ranks of his priesthood. Indeed, the first ordinations within Opus Dei only occurred in 1944 – the three non-smoking priests we mentioned earlier – and the same men became the first members of the Priestly Society of the Holy Cross. Today, there are not only just under 2,000 Opus Dei priests, but there are almost double that number who are members of the Priestly Society.

It is a standing tradition within Opus Dei that the priests are ordained from within. That means that the associates and numeraries who are already so dedicated to the organization will likely become its next generation of clergymen. This not only creates a particularly devout model of priest, but it also means that the Vatican is not able to accuse Opus Dei of stealing their priests. On becoming an Opus Dei priest, one is immediately entered into the Priestly Society. At the same time, the prelate of Opus Dei is the Society's president general. It's a regulatory quirk, however, that there is no rank within the Society. Instead, diocesan priests are still considered subject to their diocesan bishop. They are simply part of a Society built on equal footing. Once again, Escriva was very careful in the way he organized and constructed his organizations, walking the tightrope of permissiveness above the vast history, tradition, and authority of the Catholic Church.

With all of these complicated doctrinal arrangements, many people are left asking one important question: who exactly runs Opus Dei? Well, just like its relationship to the wider Catholic Church, trying to answer this question can be difficult. As might be expected from the organization that Escriva set up, the statues and canons of Opus Dei are difficult to pick apart. However, they are used to determine the internal governance of Opus Dei.

The ultimate authority within Opus Dei, unsurprisingly enough, is the prelate. This position is the natural successor to Escriva, and thus far there have only been two people who have held the post. Following the death of Escriva himself in 1975, Alvaro del Portillo was chosen as his successor. Portillo was later made a bishop by Pope John Paul II, in 1991, though he was not a bishop when he took on the prelate position. Portillo died in 1994, meaning that a vote was held and Javier Echevarria was elected to take on the position of prelate, being made a bishop the following year. Of all the positions within Opus Dei, prelate is the only one that holds a life term. The men who have held the position have also had close ties. Portillo was considered the closest collaborator of Escriva, while Echevarria was Escriva's personal secretary for many years.

Moving down the chain of command, things become more complicated. Traditionally, the Catholic Church has a clearly defined structure, with the Pope on top (in earthly terms) and then a clear organization all the way down to the local parish level. In Opus Dei, however, this is complicated by the organization's doctrine. The priests, for example, will view the prelate as their bishop. The relationship between the two positions is akin to that between a conventional Catholic diocesan priest and their respective bishop. Within the structure of Opus Dei, this is clear and simple. As soon as a priest wishes to work outside those confines, however, he finds that he must possess faculties from the respective diocesan bishop. In simple terms, Opus Dei's priests all answer to the prelate on matters related to Opus Dei. As soon as their work extends outside the organization, however, they enter into the traditional command structure of the Catholic Church, which can get quite complicated.

The prelate does not work alone, however. He is assisted by two central councils, both headquartered in Rome. The first is the General Council, the main group for the men's branch of Opus Dei, and the second is the Central Advisory Council, which deals with the women's branch of Opus Dei. Both feed advice to the prelate in order to help him make decisions. In theory, both councils are equal but are kept separate, with an almost taboo-level restriction on them holding communications with one another. As such, discussions between the two councils are handled in writing.

Since the days of Escriva, the women's council has held just as much weight as the men's when discussions are held. The prelate entertains the views and opinions of both councils and has traditionally not decimated against one side. The councils themselves are put together in similar fashion, being made up of Opus Dei members who have a history of numerous projects with youth groups, supernumeraries, and numeraries. These members rotate more often than the prelate position, so it is not uncommon for the most respected, longest-standing Opus Dei members to be invited to the position at one point or another and serve terms of eight years.

In addition to this, two important positions are the vicar-general and the secretary-general. By statute, these positions are filled with priests and are common to both branches. Between the two councils, decisions on regional delegates are put to a vote, whereby localized administrators are appointed. In Opus Dei terms, "region" is often synonymous with country, in that France and India would both be considered regions. Looking down to a regional level, the structure remains largely the same. That is to say, there is a regional vicar who is considered the authority, and he is assisted by a pair of councils, one for women and one for men. If the region is particularly large, such as the United States of America, then there are further subdivisions, named delegations, which also have the same basic structure of a vicar and two councils.

On a more general level, the regions are often split into distinct centers, of which there are over 1,750 in the world. The centers are typically the localized projection of Opus Dei. They have a director – who is not a priest – and he is assisted by a local council. The minimum requirement for a center is a director and two other members of Opus Dei. With the centers typically segregated by gender, then there is little need for male- or female-specific councils.

It can help to think of the center as the fundamental representation of Opus Dei. These buildings are the rock on which the entire organization is built, though it is not necessarily a physical place. Though many centers have lavish buildings in London or Manhattan, others have been arranged around a single residence or a workplace. The idea is that the center will assist with the organization of the means of formation. It will also provide a level of pastoral care to local members. The centers are only ever opened once Opus Dei has the permission of the bishop in the local diocese who has the right to visit the center under canon law. Once there, the diocesan bishop may carry out the traditional inspections of the tabernacle or the oratory or even the place where confession is held. Though this is permissible under Vatican rulings, it is rarely pursued. For the most part, centers are allowed to operate as they see fit.

On a grander organization level, every eight years sees the hosting of the Opus Dei General Congress. These meetings are attended by representatives from regions around the world, anywhere that Opus Dei is present. The Congresses are used for examining the work of the prelature and discussing potential directions and ideas for the future of Opus Dei. It is possible for members from around the world to present their ideas to the highest ranking member of Opus Dei, ideas which will then be discussed. Should there be a need to choose a new prelate – in the case of death, usually – then the General Congress is where the vote is held. In the past, the death of the prelate has meant the immediate calling of a General Congress in order to quickly resolve the leadership issue. The vote falls to the priests who meet the right criteria – age, length of membership, experience – and the vote is then passed along to the Pope himself for confirmation. As such, this means that the position of prelate is conferred by the Pope himself, a high honor indeed for a relatively small part of the Catholic Church. Though women are not permitted to vote, it is the female delegates who are responsible for choosing the candidates for the men to vote upon. Once again, this seems to be in line with Escriva's idea that the two sexes should be equal but should remain separate.

The organization and power structures of Opus Dei not only reveal the internal spiritual ideas that the group holds, but also looking at the history of such structures can teach us about what makes Opus Dei stand apart from many other groups. Despite their relatively small numbers, Opus Dei is treated with a huge amount of privilege within the Catholic Church. Members demand attention and seem to have carved out a niche for themselves, based chiefly on Escriva's manipulation of Catholic canon. As we will see in later chapters, this understanding forms the basis of the controversy inherent in Opus Dei. It is only through understanding the basics that we are able to learn just how strange and different Opus Dei can be. In the coming chapters, we will look closer at the more concerning, controversial, and hidden aspects of the organization.

Controversy Reigns

For the vast majority of people, the words Opus Dei only become familiar through the numerous controversial aspects of the organization. Now that we have an understanding of how the church is structured and how they approach the world, we can begin to look at how these fundamental principles will cause so much consternation among the public. From claims of extreme secrecy, to corporal mortification, to an influence in the political world, we will now examine the controversial aspects of Opus Dei and discover whether there is any truth to the rumors. In many cases, the issues surrounding Opus Dei date back to the 1940s and have been addressed by the organization on numerous occasions. However, the controversy endures.

Cloaked in Secrecy

The first issue we will address is the idea of secrecy. Opus Dei and secrets have been linked for years, with the majority of headlines involving the organization typically following the same template or pattern. There seems to be a desire on behalf of the public to learn more about Opus Dei purely because they are seen as keeping secrets from the public. There have been various claims that Opus Dei is a secret society or that its work takes place behind closed doors. But is this true?

As we are working in the confines of the English language, let's have a look back in time for the first mention of Opus Dei in the English-speaking media. An article appeared in the March edition of Time magazine in 1957, noting that three members of Opus Dei had become members in General Franco's fascist government in Spain. In the piece, Opus Dei members are referred to as "the White Masons," a hint towards their reputation for secrecy. Ironically enough, such was the nature of Franco's government that the fiercely traditional Opus Dei is mentioned in the article as having "liberal leanings," at least in comparison to the fascist regime.

The White Masons is a concept that had held true. Even is the name itself hasn't remained as popular, the idea behind it remains. The Freemasons are one of the most notorious secret societies in the world, with conspiracy theories detailing their responsibility and involvement in all manner of political machinations. It's a feeling that has been applied to Opus Dei, not only by the public at large, but also from within the Catholic Church itself. Many of these accusations can be traced by to Spain in the 1930s and 1940s when Opus Dei was competing with a number of other church organizations.

The Masonic links go as far back as the late 1930s. At the time, a number of Opus Dei members noted a drop-off in interest among young people. When they asked around, they discovered that a rumor had been circulating stating that the Opus Dei centers were emblazoned with Masonic and Kabbalistic imagery, that the communion hosts had a strange smell, that praying members conducted strange rituals including crucifixions of members in a blood-ridden style, and that Escriva himself would levitate before his congregation, hypnotizing his audience. Around this time, one of Spain's leading Jesuits accused Opus Dei of being "a secretive heretical society of a Masonic stamp."

These rumors spread through Spain like wildfire. By 1941, the fascists had set up special courts to repress the Masons and other secret societies, a move that led to Opus Dei being investigated, accused of being a "Masonic branch connected to Jewish sects." Eventually, it was archived with no effect, but that didn't stop the rumors. In 1942, a confidential report was published that described Opus Dei's secretive nature as being against the aims of the Spanish government. People wanted to know what was happening behind the closed doors of the relatively new group. Barcelona's civil governor investigated one member, demanding answers, claiming that Opus Dei was akin to a "sect of illuminati." In Valencia, they even sent a girl to be tutored by Escriva in order to uncover information, such as whether there existed secret tunnels beneath the Opus Dei center and whether it hid Masonic symbols. In certain cities, book burnings were held. Copies of *The Way*, written by Escriva, were thrown on the fires.

It didn't take long for the rumors to reach the Vatican. A report was prepared and handed to the Pope that described the "traces of a secret tendency to dominate the world with a sort of Christian Masonry." It should be noted that similar accusations were levelled at the Jesuits, as well as the Knights Templar, in the past. But the Vatican did nothing. Despite the furor over the secretive approach of Opus Dei, no charges or allegations were ever formally levelled. Instead, rumors and stories circulated about what happened inside the Opus Dei centers.

Over the years, these accusations have resurfaced. The Vatican wrote to Escriva in 1971 and requested a list of all Opus Dei members, as they were concerned about rumors that the organization was "infiltrating" the Vatican. Escriva complied. Such accusations bounced back and forth between Catholic and secular spheres, with both sides concerned about Opus Dei's secrecy. In 1986, the Italian parliament mentioned Opus Dei in an investigation into the influence of secret societies. It was eight months before the organization was cleared by Oscar Luigi Scalfaro, himself a staunch Catholic man. In defense of Opus Dei's supposed secrecy, Scalfaro pointed out that the organization's Italian headquarters were stationed in Milan, and he gave the address and telephone number for their information desk. This, he suggested, was not expected from a secret society.

This contrasted with the findings of a Swiss court a few years later, when an Opus Dei-related educational group found themselves in a dispute with a newspaper. The court found that Opus Dei was indeed a "covertly" operating "secret organization." In 1996, a parliamentary commission in France included Opus Dei on a list of 172 sects (or dangerous religious movements) that operated in France. Though a number of French and Italian bishops protested, the Vatican made no official comment. Two months later, however, Pope John Paul II named a church in Rome after Escriva. However, these claims of secrecy are not confined to the past. Still today, people view membership in Opus Dei as being akin to being a member of a secret society.

Perhaps the reason why the secrecy issue has become so central to criticism of Opus Dei is because of the inability to discern membership with any great accuracy. Across the world, and in Spain especially, there are many Opus Dei members who work in conventional offices, progressing along traditional career paths.

Occasionally, you could be shocked to discover that your normal, competent coworker is actually an Opus Dei member and you never had any idea. This person might not go home every night to a family, as you do, but he instead travels home to the local center, prays in silence, unclasps the cilice belt that has been cutting into his leg for hours, and then commences his weekly ritual of whipping himself while praying. To many people, the idea that their co-workers could be involved in so alien a lifestyle is shocking. To some, it is unwelcome.

On a surface level, there seems to be little way to tell if a person is an Opus Dei member. Being involved in the organization is no great secret, and many members will be happy to share. Others, however, have become aware of the rumors and reputation and wish to keep their membership a secret. Unlike many other Christian denominations, Opus Dei members do not pride themselves on lapel pins and bumper stickers. Such an issue has led to the spreading of many rumors.

In Spain, particularly, there is a list of ways in which you can supposedly spot an Opus Dei member. One such theory is that members favor Atkinson's cologne, said to be Escriva's personal choice. Similarly, there is a rumor that Opus Dei businessmen can be identified by a missing button on the sleeve of their suit jacket. Another is that members smoke Ducados cigarettes, perhaps a reference to the tale of the three priests and an effort to fit in. Speaking to actual members, however, these ideas are quickly put to bed.

There are some theories that are a little less out there. Some say you can spot Opus Dei members because they will own a small statue of a donkey. It's certainly not obligatory, but many Opus Dei centers do have donkey statues, a common symbol throughout the organization, with Escriva having compared himself to the donkey that carried Christ into Jerusalem. In a similar vein, "Pax" is a common greeting between Opus Dei members, to which the correct reply is "in aeternum." This is not a foolproof method of identification, however, as those who use it will need to know that the other is certainly in the organization and will often simply avoid doing so around people who are not Opus Dei members.

Indeed, most Opus Dei members adhere to what is known as "discretion." People do not advertise their Opus Dei membership in too brazen a fashion, partly due to a desire to retain the secular nature of the organization. Members are not meant to be like those in other religious orders; they don't want to appear religious. As well as this, Escriva warned against those who might try to use their Opus Dei membership to advance their careers, so many choose to not advertise the fact at all. Escriva also preached the idea of "collective humility," meaning that Opus Dei as an organization should not seek out self-aggrandizement, something which was written directly into the constitution of the order and forbids the wearing of "distinctive insignia" and other such advertisements.

There's even a canonical reason as to why Opus Dei might be more withdrawn about membership. During the period between 1947 and 1982, the organization was classified by the Vatican as a "secular institute." This meant that it was to be treated as being outside of religious life. By 1950, changes in the regulations meant that members were technically in violation of the Church's laws. So as not to draw attention to the fact, many of the upper echelons of Opus Dei decided that discretion might be the best option. In the modern day, Opus Dei's reputation might be reason enough for people to keep quiet.

It's also worth noting that Opus Dei members are not alone in their discretion. There are many organizations within the Catholic Church that do not openly broadcast their membership. Among these are the Missionaries of the Kingship of Christ, the Community of Stain John, the Crusaders of Saint Mary, and the Father Kolbe Missionaries of Immaculata. Few of these groups have anything like the notoriety of Opus Dei, but their practices could be described as similarly secretive.

But the secrecy does not just apply to membership. Over the last few decades, the "secret statutes" have garnered a great deal of attention. These statutes are the Vatican laws that have been approved by the Pope and that govern Opus Dei as an organization. As a rule, access to these documents is forbidden to the majority of people. A quick Google search will seemingly confirm this, with many websites clamoring to discuss the hidden statutes and what could possibly be contained within.

This is not entirely true, however. In 1982, a book titled *The Canonical Path of Opus Dei* was published by the organization and contained a copy – in full – of the statutes. There is a problem for most people, though, in that the documents were published in their original form. That is to say, they were written in Latin. Opus Dei has never officially offered a translation of the statutes, so all inquiries to see such documents are directed to a set of regulations that most people cannot read. Even then, translations can be difficult. An unauthorized, unofficial translation may interpret laws slightly differently than Opus Dei's original. Many people have seen this as Opus Dei's dodging of the requests to see their governing laws. According to the organization, the fact that the statutes are Vatican-created documents means that it falls on the Vatican to offer a translation. Again, people have seen this as dodging the issue.

In addition to the "secret statutes," there are other internal documents that are definitely kept hidden. There are many internal publications, magazines, and leaflets that are designed for internal reading only. Many of these, Opus Dei argues, need to be kept within the organization due to the fact that they might be misinterpreted without the correct context. While come critics have suggested that these internal publications – such as *Cronica* and *Noticias* – are used to propagandize and rewrite the history of the organization, Opus Dei themselves suggest that these pieces are simply private collections of members' memories and thoughts, not intended for public consumption. Indeed, it is not impossible to obtain a copy of these texts and many have made their way out of the various Opus Dei centers around the world.

Regardless of how much information is allowed to leak out of the Opus Dei centers around the world, people will remain curious about certain elements of the organization. Often, Opus Dei's notoriety feeds into this. People become curious about the organization and hope to find out more, only to discover a blocked path in their way. This naturally makes them even more curious, to the point of being accusatory. As we shall see in the following sections, however, withholding information might be the least secret, least strange aspect of Opus Dei.

Pain Threshold

If you ask most people what they know about Opus Dei, chances are they will give you an answer focused on mortification. Thanks to the huge popularity of Dan Brown's book, the Da Vinci Code, and the subsequent film, many people in the English speaking world first heard of the organization through a fictional character. One of the most shocking traits of the Opus Dei monk in the book – at least, for the uninitiated – is the way in which he inflicts pain upon himself as an act of prayer. Though Dan Brown's book has been criticized in many circles (for many reasons), this much is true: mortification has long been one of the strangest parts of Opus Dei and is certainly one of the most notorious.

Mortification, as it is understood here, involves inflicting physical harm upon oneself in order to "tame the flesh" and bring the human experience closer to that of Jesus Christ. But before we continue with this section, we should clear up one important fact. Mortification is only practiced by a small percentage of the Opus Dei membership, and even in this case, it is often far tamer than depicted in many works of fiction. However, that does not stop many of the more incendiary details from being repeated in the main stream media. But what is the truth?

Bold claims about Opus Dei can be traced all the way back to its roots. As early as the 1930s and 1940s, Escriva and his new group were accused of many crimes, including heresy, Masonry, Kabbalah, ritualism, and even having secret tunnels under their centers. But at the time, few people saw fit to criticize the practice of mortification. At the time, it was a recognized part of many spiritualist beliefs.

Just like the tools of Opus Dei's mortification, other Church groups had similar devices. The hair shirt is the name given to one such device, a rough cloth garment inlaid with barbed chains and worn beneath the regular clothes. The hair shirt was demonstrative of many Catholic practices from before the 20th Century, the point being to inflict discomfort. Pope Paul VI was known to use a hair shirt, for example, right up until the day of his death. For monks during the 1930s and the 1940s, the time when Opus Dei came into being, such a practice was commonplace for monks. In addition, the whip known as the flagellum was another common tool, with Church scholars as far back as the 10th Century praising its pain-inflicting abilities.

For some Opus Dei members, tools such as the cilice (the strap wrapped around the thigh) are much like the rosary. Neither were invented by members of Opus Dei. But such comments do little to address the fact that mortification devices are not only out of favor, but are seen by the rest of society as being destructive and harmful. Thus, it's little surprise that such antiquated and poorly thought of practices should attract attention to Opus Dei. To those who are critical of Opus Dei, such behavior is an example of the organization's inhumane approach to religion. Though for those who admire the group, it should be noted that Opus Dei's refusal to bow to modern tastes is commendable.

Trying to understand mortification as it pertains to the individual members can be tough. Though all members of Opus Dei technically take part, only around 30% are involved in the more headline-grabbing kinds of self-inflicted violence. For the supernumeraries, mostly laymen and female members, whipping oneself or wearing a cilice is hardly ever done. Instead, they're too busy with families and children, using their working lives to sanctify their relationship with God. Often, they can have an entirely different form of mortification. This might amount to chores, such as doing the washing up when it isn't your turn or doing a small favor for someone.

In terms of the remaining 30% of Opus Dei members, however, there is little question that the mortification practices are violent in nature and intended to cause pain. Let's take a closer look at some of the most common:

The **Cilice**, mentioned already, is a spiked chain. Members wear it bound around the upper thigh for around two hours every day (excluding Sundays, feast days, and other notable days). It is sharp enough to leave visible pin pricks in the flesh once removed, which can add up to noticeable scarring over time. Due to the nature of the device, most numeraries prefer to wear it in the privacy of the Opus Dei center. When wearing it in day-to-day life, it can be a visible sign, something that would contravene the idea of discretion. There are reports of members who do wear the cilice during everyday life, with these individuals often claiming that it can remind the wearer of its presence during difficult times, providing extra concentration, focus, and an affirmation of one's relationship with God.

The **Discipline**, also mentioned elsewhere in this book, is the famous whip used by Opus Dei members. There is often a lot of confusion as to the size and nature of the device, but it is not the heavy, thick strip of leather that most people expect. Instead, it's more like a thin cord, often made using macramé-weaving methods. Typically, it will be held in one hand and used during prayer time. For the duration of a prayer such as a Hail Mary or an Our Father, the Opus Dei member will whip themselves across either the back or the buttocks at regular intervals. If a member so desires, they can speak to their priest and ask permission to use the discipline more regularly.

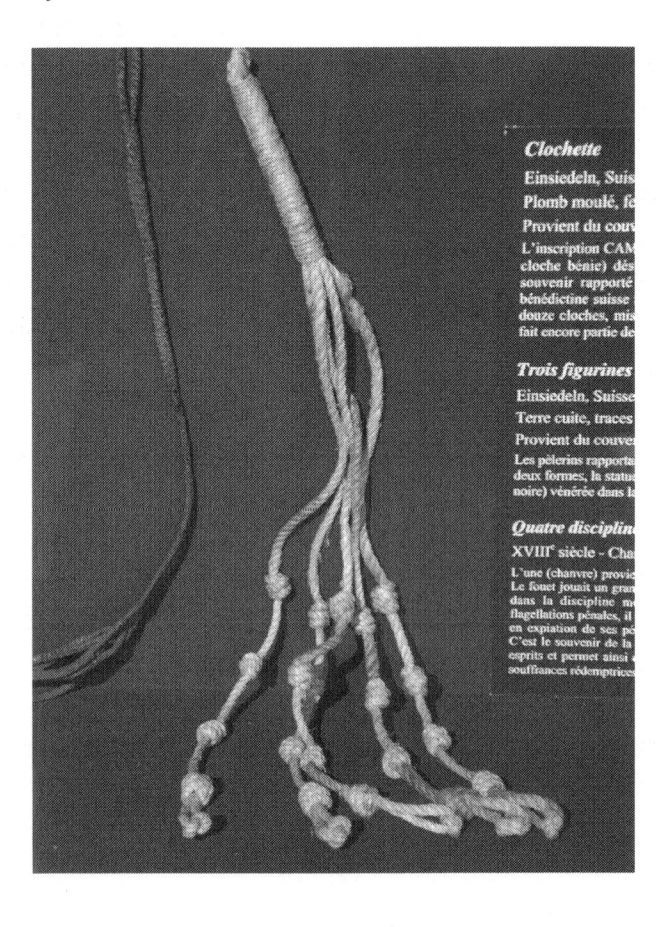

Sleeping arrangements can often be a part of the mortification practices. For female numeraries, this can involve uncomfortable sleeping arrangements, placing a thin but hard board over the top of a normal mattress and forgoing the use of pillows at least one night a week. For their male equivalents, this can be a case of sleeping on a floor for one night a week or similarly going without a pillow. Though much less attention-grabbing than other mortification efforts, these practices are widely used throughout Opus Dei and can provide high levels of discomfort.

In terms of eating, it's possible to practice corporal mortification even during meal times. This could be something small such as forgoing the use of sugar or milk in one's coffee, choosing not to have dessert or a second course, and other variations on this theme. There are also designated fast days, on which Opus Dei members will refrain from eating within certain parameters. Theoretically, such practices should apply to all Catholics, though few are as strict as Opus Dei members when it comes to observing the traditions.

Silence is also a means of practicing corporal mortification. Every night, many Opus Dei members will enter into a personal examination of their own conscience. During this time, numeraries are often encouraged to stay in complete silence right through until the following morning's mass has been completed. This self-imposed silence is just another way in which members deny themselves privileges and remind themselves of their relationship with God.

There are also many other practices that have come in and out of fashion among Opus Dei members. In the 1980s, for example, many numeraries were encouraged to partake in cold showers. This was eventually phased out, though rumors have remained that Opus Dei centers do not have hot running water. This is untrue, but it is an example of how the ideas of mortification can feed into the social comprehension of Opus Dei.

So what of Escriva? Did the Opus Dei founder approve of the practice of mortification? There are a number of references to these kinds of practices in Escriva's writing. At one point in *The Way*, he recalls the ways in which saints such as Francis of Assisi, Benedict, and Bernard all exposed themselves to uncomfortable situations. Elsewhere, he describes the human body as the "enemy" and asks the reader why they treat this enemy "so softly." It's an idea Escriva returns to later, writing in *The Forge* that "what has been through the flesh, the flesh should pay back."

As well as his writings, there are examples from Escriva's own life that point toward him approving of such practices. Stories have been told by biographers of the man's private praying sessions, which would often describe in the detail the thick sound of the blows against his skin. By the end, the witness remembers, the floor was "covered with blood." But whether Escriva recommended these practices to his followers is much debated. It seems, at least, that Escriva was leading the way in terms of mortification, even if he did not see it as an essential part of Opus Dei.

It's a point of practice in Opus Dei to suggest that Escriva is not a figure to be emulated. Now officially a saint in the Catholic Church, there's little need for every single member to believe that they could possibly emulate Escriva's own piousness. There are writings from Escriva that explicitly state that those practicing mortification should never do so if it directly endangers their lives or "embitters [their] characters." Indeed, unlike Escriva's own floor-bloodying efforts, he explicitly states that the cornerstone of penitence is love.

So if mortification is not essential to membership in Opus Dei, then why do so many people practice it still? If you listen to the criticism and conspiracies surrounding the organization, then it can be easy to overlook the supposed justification for carrying out such rituals. There is a spiritual goal behind mortification, one which members say is overlooked by the more fantastical, tabloid nature of much Opus Dei coverage in the media. Running a mile, they suggest, might bring about far more hardship and pain for people than the wearing of a cilice.

Mortification has been a part of Catholicism from long before the arrival of Opus Dei. Traditionally, it was part of the process of training people to live virtuously and devoutly. Known as asceticism, the practice has become a hallmark of the way Catholicism has been taught over the centuries. Gradually, the body is trained to endure hardships. These can come in many forms, and as we have already seen, they go in and out of fashion on a regular basis. It might help to view mortification as a form of spiritual exercise, gradually working oneself into better shape. It's not exclusively Catholic and could theoretically be practiced by a Muslim, a Sikh, or an atheist. It's even seen often in day-to-day life. For example, a parent withholding dessert from a poorly behaved child would fit the bill. What makes the practice particularly Christian, however, is the view that mortification is a response to sin.

When a sin has been committed, it's possible to use mortification in order to revive a sense of penitence. It's meant to kindle in the person a desire to rectify a situation, to make up for their sin. There's an idea that mortification is the person physically reminding themselves that sin causes wounds. These wounds are in the sinner, in the person they have sinned against, and in God. That's not to say that comforts and pleasant things are inherently sinful, but rather than the acknowledgement that these things are good. Conversely then, denying them to oneself is all the greater because of this. It's a sign of regret, showing God that you're sorry that you've sinned, and that you're resolved not to do the same again.

There's a second, deeper, spiritual level. Through mortification, a person is able to unite themselves with the suffering of Jesus Christ. In particular, the suffering that Christ endured during the crucifixion is replicated (on a much smaller scale) in order to draw a person closer to their deity. There's a degree of atonement, sharing the burden of pain taht forms a large part of the theological message of the New Testament.

For celibates, this kind of mortification is seen as a chance for them to "give themselves" to God in as complete a manner as possible. For the majority of Catholics, this is a silent, internal process. The things to overcome are often abstract, such as hatred or pride. The difference with Opus Dei is that they are able to make these challenges physical, translating the same kind of theological issues present for most Catholics into something that is far more sensational when viewed without context.

But it's not only Opus Dei who practice mortification to this degree. Even some of the most famous Catholics of the last hundred years have been mortification advocates. Both Mother Teresa and Padre Pio were known to wear a cilice and used the discipline at one time or another. Both are now considered saints and neither were Opus Dei members. There is a community of nuns (the Discalced Carmelite Convent of Saint Teresa) in the Italian city of Livorno who construct mortification tools and sell them to the Catholic community at large. Again, they are not associated with Opus Dei in anything beyond the occasional business relationship.

So, in addition to Opus Dei, orders such as the Discalced Carmelites, the Franciscan Brothers, the Sisters of the Immaculate Conception, the Mother of the Church Monastery, and many more groups practice forms of mortification. These organizations exist all across the world, though few garner as many headlines as Opus Dei. The practice – in its more severe and more benign forms – is likely far more common in the Catholic Church than many people would care to imagine.

Despite this, the practice of mortification has inspired some of the most stinging criticisms of Opus Dei. One of these is former numeraries Sharon Clasen, who has left the organization and become of the best known writers on Opus Dei and its practices. To Clasen, Opus Dei is a cult. Her experiences in the organization have left a bitter, regretful, and painful taste in her mouth. One of her biggest criticisms is focused on the practice of mortification and how it affects people. The practices, she says, are indication of the "annihilation of the self" that Opus Dei is attempting to symbolically achieve.

Clasen can recall the time, shortly after she became a member, when she was handed a little blue pouch. Inside were her cilice and her discipline, ready for her to begin using. It was the first time she had seen either device. After three years of wearing the cilice and using the discipline, she had even been given classes and lessons on how to respond to people who might question her about them. These answers were along the familiar Opus Dei lines, suggesting that mortification was akin to heavy exercise. As well as this, rumors spread through the centers of how Escriva himself had practiced mortification, suggesting that he had fitted his discipline with broken glass and razor blades. According to Clasen, the idea behind spreading these rumors was to encourage a similar level of "devoutness" among numeraries.

She goes on to tell a story about how she attempted to follow in the potentially mythical footsteps of Escriva. While still at the center, Clasen found herself some safety pins. She opened them out, exposing the sharp points, and fitted them to the discipline she had been given. Using the modified whip, Clasen said her prayers. It was something she only attempted a few times, though it was far from unheard of among the Opus Dei community. Though she has since left the organization, the sight of a cilice can be enough to bring Sharon Clasen close to tears. She is not alone.

Another ex-member who has been critical of Opus Dei's ideas about mortification is John Roche. An Irishman who joined the organization in 1959, Roche spent fourteen years in the church, including time spent in an Opus Dei center in Kenya. While official Opus Dei information states that the more extreme versions of mortification is a rare occurrence and only limited, Roche confirms Clasen's version of events, suggesting that painful practices are used with regularity and often to extremes.

What is perhaps worse is the way in which those who do not practice mortification are treated by their fellow church members. Those who are deemed not sufficiently invested in the practice of physical mortification can sometimes be criticized openly. As stories circulate about how Escriva drove himself to extremes of mortification, those who don't show willingness to follow in his footsteps can feel as though they are being ostracized and targeted. Even if this is not official policy in the organization, the reports of its widespread nature are damning.

Another former member critical of Opus Dei is Agustina Lopez de los Mozos, who now runs a website that is designed to spread her views on the organization. Agustina was a numerary assistant for eight years, from her late teens until her mid-twenties. She was introduced to the cilice a short time after requesting admission. Though it was still a short time before she was given her own device, it's telling that the mortification practices are rarely revealed until after eager young recruits are firmly within the grips of the organization.

According to Agustina's story, the thinking regarding the cilice within Opus Dei is that the tighter it is tied, the greater one's "generosity" is held to be. It's almost competitive in the organization, with everyone eager to prove their devotion and relationship with God. Thus, more and more people tie the cilice tighter, wearing it for longer than the official recommendations might suggest. Even though the time limit is given as two hours a day, many people go beyond this. Many people wear a cilice every day, alternating legs to give their wounds a chance to heal.

Under the official prescription, the cilice should not break the skin. Agustina's experience, however, describes how extended periods of wearing the device would result in her removing bits of skin after every session, leaving behind wounds that would often take days to heal. Before they even had a chance to close, the wounds would be exposed to another cilice session only a short time later. When Agustina tried to wear the cilice around her waist – hoping that it would be less visible and less painful – she was admonished by the numerary who had given it to her.

When asked for comment about these punishing practices, Opus Dei officials have described the advice given to the above members as "errors." But there is little doubt that these kinds of practices do happen, and accordingly attract more and more attention to the church. With the sometimes shocking degrees of self-afflicted-violence that are evident among members, this attention is perhaps overwhelmingly negative. In the defense of Opus Dei, they did not invent, nor do they claim any exclusivity over violent mortification practices. However, there seems to be a very evident culture within the organization that proliferates and spreads practices that endanger the health of members. However, while these actions might get more of the attention in the press, there are greater structural problems that exist within Opus Dei. Aside from the headline-grabbing nature of mortification, it is the subject matters of the next sections that should cause greater consternation.

Women's Place

It's impossible to deny the fact that the Catholic Church has long has a troubled history of gender equality. A quick glance through the opening passages of the Bible is all one needs to confirm this, with the entire premise of original sin being predicated on the easily tempted nature of the world's first woman. Throughout the centuries, the Church's patriarchal stance has long been a reflection of a similar stance across all of Western civilization. Though there have undoubtedly been women within the Church who have done a great deal for female suffrage, it is only in recent times that the Church has purposefully made a move towards being inclusive.

However, this book is not about the history of the Catholic Church. Just as Opus Dei often reflects the best and the worst aspects of traditional Catholic views, their treatment of women is one of the most criticized dimensions of the organization as a whole. Opus Dei's treatment and views regarding women are often one of the unmentioned issues. With mortification grabbing all of the headlines, this gender inequality can often be forced to take a backseat. But how big of an issue is it?

There has long been a sensation among those on the periphery of Opus Dei that the organization hides some hostility towards women. It's often an unspoken sensation, something that rumbles beneath the surface. For some, it is an extension of a centuries-old patriarchy, while for others it is a reflection of the group's fear of sexuality and the female gender. This, they say, has translated into a view of women that treats them as second class citizens, even if they are Opus Dei members.

Looking at the raw figures for Opus Dei, this might seem strange. At least 55%, a solid majority, of the members are female. For those sympathetic to Opus Dei, the argument is that the Church's two systems of governance – a branch for men and a branch for women – guarantees a systemic equality. The female members, they argue, receive the same theological, spiritual teaching, and formation as their male counterparts. Indeed, in certain regions, there are women who hold positions that would place them on a higher administrative rank than men. But still, there is the feeling that Opus Dei does not view both genders to be equal.

Like all matters pertaining to Opus Dei, it can help to think about what Escriva considered to be the correct path. On the whole, his discussions on the matter seem to be in favor of permitting women the exact same rights and privileges as men. For example, he faced criticism in some circles for his encouragement that women should study for theology degrees. While he seemed to come down heavily on the side of equal rights, however, Escriva's views were not entirely conclusive. In some respects, he admitted to a belief that a "distinction" should be retained regarding the juridical capacity for receiving holy orders. He did admit, on another occasion, that without women, Opus Dei's work would collapse. But despite what their founder proclaimed and despite seeming attempts to provide women with an institutional (but separate) equality, there still persists the same notion that women are not on the same standing as men.

One of the best places to start when examining this issue is the numerary assistants. These are women who have devoted their whole lives to Opus Dei and often to carrying out the domestic care duties associated with running one of the organization's centers. Cooking, cleaning, handling the laundry – the women's position within the organization seems to tally with the traditional patriarchal view of the housewife. In creating the position, the founders of Opus Dei seem to have transplanted the inherent inequality of 1930s Spain society and institutionalized it. The result was an official position of women in which they were tasked with domestic chores. While the rest of Western society seems to have moved forward with regards to women's place in the "domestic sphere," Opus Dei has not.

However, this role is not one given to all women in Opus Dei. Of the 47,000 female members, only 4,000 are actually numerary assistants. The vast majority are actually supernumeraries, meaning that they will likely enjoy a life outside of the Opus Dei centers. This might mean that they are lawyers, doctors, or possibly even homemakers for their own families. But often these members are among the least visible. As is the case with mortification, it's the minority within the organization who seem to garner the most attention. Perhaps that is because many people not involved with Opus Dei would be shocked to discover that the organization proudly enjoys an entire class of membership (exclusively female) whose job seems to be entirely involving domestic service.

But that's not the end of the criticism. Those who are unimpressed by Opus Dei have commented on the fact that the recruitment of numerary assistants seems to draw exclusively from society's poorer classes. In doing so, these underprivileged women are told that such a role is the vocation given to them by God and that they should relinquish any ideas of marriage and children. Instead, they should focus on serving Opus Dei (and thus serving God). Once they have been recruited, these women often work incredibly long hours. Accordingly, the critics suggest that Opus Dei is taking advantage of these women, using religion almost as a force of cheap, patriarchy-approved labor.

Of course, such a summation often dismisses the wishes of the women who possess an honest dedication to Opus Dei and view their work as a numerary assistant as a form of devotion. To these people, it is an honor to work in the Opus Dei centers. But such an honor is one that is available only to women, bequeathed upon them by a male-orientated order. In line with Escriva's original visions, the role of the numerary assistants is one that is an archaic relic of Opus Dei's moment of creation, one out of place in the modern world.

Another familiar Opus Dei argument in favor of the status quo is that the arrangement plays on natural predilections. To Opus Dei, it seems only natural that women enjoy an "instinctive aptitude" for domestic chores such as cooking and cleaning. Furthermore, it is an aptitude that the majority of men do not possess. The argument is just as antiquated as the arrangement itself, though it seems to be one that is routinely made. The position of the numerary assistants does not seem to be going anywhere. As Opus Dei becomes more famous for embodying the traditional conservatism of the Catholic Church, such positions are part and parcel of their success. To them, the notion of a male numerary assistant is absurd. There exists – at all times – a reluctance to change any part of the organization from the blueprint which was laid down by Escriva himself. As society moves further and further forwards, Opus Dei is increasingly left behind.

But as well as the numerary assistants, the desire to keep both genders separate for as long as possible permeates much of the Opus Dei structure. As much as possible, the organization hopes to keep men and women separate. There are separate centers (where possible) for men and women, with even shared buildings having separate entrances. During events, there is separation. During retreats, there is separation. Schools are not only exclusive to male or female students, but the faculty is also divided along gender lines. The desire to keep men and women separate is near constant.

There are many stories about the lengths that church members go to in order to avoid interaction between men and women. We've mentioned a tendency to put everything in writing when communicating between male and female branches of the organization, but many members and ex-members have personal stories about how extreme this notion can be. One story tells of how an IT technician was told by Opus Dei members that there should be two separate phone lines installed in the building, as well as separate computer systems. Even though it was set to cost twice as much to install a computer and phone system for each gender, Opus Dei were happy to commission the work.

To those outside of the confines of Opus Dei, this separation seems somewhat bizarre but mostly harmless. Catholics, even traditionally inclined Catholics, have noted their amusement at Opus Dei's stance on separation. As per usual, the organization defends its actions by citing Escriva, not wanting to alter the structure as the founder saw it. A reluctance to modernize, in this instance, has drawn criticism from feminist organizations as well as secular groups. But when it comes to separation, the reaction to Opus Dei is typically one of pity and confusion rather than revulsion. It is widely accepted outside of the organization that Opus Dei possesses an inherent issue with women. Occasionally, this is acknowledged and excused by Opus Dei itself, but it seems unlikely to be an issue that they are likely to address in the near future. Until then, the role of the numerary assistants and the extent of the gender separation is likely to remain evidence of the systemic, institutional misogyny that exists within Opus Dei.

Follow the Money

In criminal investigations, there is an old mantra repeated like gospel. If you want to find out who is pulling the strings, follow the money. For Opus Dei and those investigating the organization's strange place within the religious landscape, this mantra is particularly telling. Despite their relatively small size and membership numbers, Opus Dei is renowned for its somewhat astonishing financial muscle. To say it punches above its weight in financial terms would be an understatement. So, following the old police saying, if we want to find out why Opus Dei seems to be both controversial and important, then we should follow the money. The only problem is, tracing the organization's funding can be incredibly tough.

There have been rumors since the 1960s that Opus Dei has long been a "major player" in the market for Eurodollars. This is only a small part of the back story concerning Opus Dei and their finances, but it forms a good starting point. Why would a nominally conservative Catholic denomination be speculating on currency markets? One investigator – Canadian journalist Robert Hutchinson – wrote a book on the matter. He could recall being perplexed by the appearance that Opus Dei had a greater value of assets than General Motors. Whenever Opus Dei is confronted with the suggestion that it might be dabbling in such financial markets, Hutchinson reports a constant stream of shrugged shoulders and bewildered denials. For the Canadian, this was enough to prompt comparisons between the modern Opus Dei and the Crusader-era Knights Templar, a Catholic organization that had one of the first international banking organizations in the world.

However, much of Hutchinson's work is speculation. His investigations have yet to uncover the single piece of evidence that ties together the entire picture of Opus Dei's finances, leaving him to speculate on the values and nature of the organization's portfolio. His writing, though, reflects a widespread belief. Even at the most liberal end of the estimation spectrum, Opus Dei's holdings have been said to total $2.8 billion. While only a fraction of General Motors annual revenues, it's still leaps and bounds beyond what many would expect for a religious group less than a million people strong.

There has been a noted decision within the Catholic Church during the 20th Century to ally themselves with the poor and disenfranchised. Since the convening of Vatican II and the creation of the "Gaudium et Spes" document, the Church has tried to actively distance itself from its lavish, rich past. Thus, once again, Opus Dei is more indicative of the more traditional qualities of the Church. In this case, it would be the extreme wealth concentrated in a relatively small group.

It's an issue that serves to highlight the difference in how Opus Dei perceives itself and how it is perceived by the outside world. If you believe spokespeople for it, then Opus Dei has no desire to become a financial heavyweight and would much rather own as little as possible. This, they say, would detach them from Earthly wealth. But does this hold up to scrutiny?

In Rome, Opus Dei owns and operates their central offices, split into men and women's sections. The annual operating budget for the buildings is $2.7 million. This might pale in comparison to the $260 million needed to run the Vatican each year, but then Opus Dei's offices are not a global tourist destination, nor do they house some of the greatest works of art created by a person, nor do the administrators have to cater to a billion plus people around the world.

Opus Dei's headquarters might seem like an expensive outlay, but they do not own all of their property around the world. Sometimes they lease, sometimes they rent. Sometimes, the buildings are owned by local churches or shell companies. In a similar sense, the organization's more secular endeavors – the schools, universities, and other enterprises – are often owned and attributed to lay people. These are members of Opus Dei, and the enterprises are operated as Opus Dei officially sanctioned endeavors, but they are not technically owned by it. While Opus Dei insists that this allows them to remain secular and independent from the vast wealth needed to run such matters, critics have suggested that such practices simply allow Opus Dei to hide the true extent of their assets.

There has long been a dispute about the purview of Opus Dei. The organization itself maintains that any business ventures owned and operated by its members will be entirely their own enterprises. Opus Dei might provide a spiritual guidance or doctrine that helps guide members through the world of business, but the organization will remain separate at all times. This is an idea that has been outright dismissed by critics such as Michael Walsh. Walsh suggests that distinguishing between members' businesses and Opus Dei's own is useless, listing a number of reasons.

First, he claims, all profits made by numeraries' businesses will accrue to Opus Dei anyway. Even supernumeraries who own businesses are often pressured into giving up most of their profits. Second, Walsh believes that every major business decision taken by an Opus Dei member will be discussed at length with the director of their local center before starting. The communication channels are totally open, and the organization always knows what its members are doing. These are accusations that Opus Dei denies.

Due to the insistence on secularity in Opus Dei, getting even the most basic financial information from the organization is sometimes almost impossible. There has been a suggestion from within it that the secular reasoning is not the only one for Opus Dei putting its businesses in members' hands. Without creating a central "pool" of Opus Dei funds, there is nothing that could be mismanaged or misused. Doing so limits Opus Dei's exposure to potential trouble. Spreading the organization's supposed wealth across a large body of trusted individuals is a form of protectionism, from both financial misappropriation and investigative critics.

Part of the reason as to why people struggle to believe Opus Dei's claims of dedication to poverty lies in the properties they use. Centers can be found in wealthy, upscale neighborhoods, and it's not uncommon for such buildings to be lavishly decorated. Even if those inside might be taking cold showers and sleeping on the floor, the outward appearance – the customer-facing part – of Opus Dei is resolutely wealthy. Though it might counter with claims that not all centers are in wealthy neighborhoods or that the centers themselves are actually owned by a member, it's difficult to satisfactorily explain why it seems to have such untold resources at its disposal.

There seems little doubt that Opus Dei is a wealthy organization. The group contains members who control businesses worth a huge amount while still fundraising and collecting revenue themselves. It's an organization who has its own multimillion-dollar investment portfolio, as well as assets scattered around the world. We know that there is a huge amount of money involved, but tracking it down can be difficult. Opus Dei is very careful about limiting their exposure. As such, we should begin to look at the ways in which their wealth is transferred into influence. Through a variety of means, Opus Dei has risen up as one of the major players in the world of Catholicism and religion as a whole. While we might never be able to follow the money directly to the source, we can track down the places where that money is most influential.

The Church and the Government

Throughout this book, we have examined the differences of Opus Dei when compared to the traditional Catholic Church. To pretend that they are distant relations would be a lie. Opus Dei and the Vatican have always been close. In this section, we will explore their relationship.

The majority of this section will focus on recent history. We should start by establishing a few facts. First, during the pontificate of Pope John Paul II, no other group seemed to be as approved by the Church as Opus Dei. It was during this time that it became a papal prelature, and a short time later, Escriva was made a saint. Second, Opus Dei officials have been instrumental in shaping recent Vatican doctrine. In 2001, for example, a well-known Opus Dei priest was among those behind "Dominus Iesus," a document that described the "gravely deficient" situation other religions found themselves in with respect to Christianity. Third, reports in 2004 highlighted the controversy in comments that were attributed to Pope John Paul II. Upon seeing the film the *Passion of the Christ*, the then-Pope is reported to have said, "It is as it was," a major endorsement. The controversy stems from both whether this was actually said and the fact that the film's assistant director is not only an Opus Dei member, but was also personally baptized by Pope John Paul II when he was still the Bishop of Rome. These incidents, along with many others, amount to give an idea of the amount of power and influence Opus Dei enjoys within the walls of Vatican City.

Taking a broader look at the picture, and connections begin to emerge. It's possible to draw links between Opus Dei, the Vatican, and any number of conservative political causes. In the majority of incidents concerning the Church, it's not uncommon to find that Opus Dei members are at the core of the side closest linked to traditional, conservative beliefs. Any time the Church veers in this direction, it's easy to see why people believe this is Opus Dei's influence shining through.

There are even rumors that have persisted around Vatican City that Opus Dei is mounting a plan to take over many internal Vatican organizations, including the Vatican Radio broadcast service. Currently, the radio station costs a great deal of money to broadcast to hundreds of millions of people every day. Opus Dei could swoop in as a financial backer and take on the costs itself, in exchange for a tighter control over the content that is broadcast. There are similar rumors about taking over Vatican-backed universities and schools. Opus Dei has already enacted a similar plan by taking over convents and seminaries that need financial help. All of the rumors are denied by Opus Dei, but they will not seem to go away.

Though he is now deceased, the bond between Opus Dei and Pope John Paul II is seen by many as having been the launching pad for much of Opus Dei's recent success. The personal prelature is the most famous example of this relationship and drove many English-language press outlets to investigate further. John Paul II spoke officially on Opus Dei a number of times, always positively. He seemed to approve of much of the organization's work and was an admirer of Escriva. It's a close relationship that continued after the death of one Pope and into the reign of the next. Though it might be too early to discern the current Pope's relationship with Opus Dei, we can be confident that little happens within the Church without the organization's approval.

Having existed for close to two millennia, it's no surprise to learn that there are multiple cliques and groups within the wider Catholic Church. Whenever a new cardinal is elected, it's common for priests in Rome to ask about his parish. They don't mean the area he administers, but rather which friends he has within the Vatican. Opus Dei is one of the growing groups.

Looking at it from afar, Opus Dei involvement seems to be limited. Officially, there are less than ten high-ranking Vatican officials who are Opus Dei members. At the time of writing, there are two cardinals and twenty bishops who are officially Opus Dei members. But it is impossible to quantify those who are sympathetic to the Opus Dei cause or consider themselves traditionalists in some degree. With Opus Dei being thought to represent the best of the latter, conservative movements within the Church are often associated with Opus Dei to some degree. For example, there are a further fourteen bishops who are members of the Priestly Society of the Holy Cross. If you'd like to know more about who has connections and sympathies to Opus Dei, then a quick flick through the *Annuario* (the annual Vatican yearbook) is often enough. Again and again, the entire suggestion seems to revert back to the idea of the White Masonry.

The personal prelature, the canonization of Opus Dei's founder, the presence of Opus Dei cardinals and bishops, and the personal relationship between the organization and the last few Popes certainly points towards Opus Dei possessing a special privilege in the Catholic Church. Indeed, the process of making Escriva a saint was considered especially quick, with just twenty-seven years passing between his death and his canonization. As a point of comparison, it took Joan of Arc around six hundred years to achieve the same. The cost of turning Escriva into a saint cost more than a million dollars, and not everyone within the Catholic Church approved of the canonization, with some voices concerned that critical witnesses to the process were not heard. In some cases, it has been said that Opus Dei's influence and power ensured the process was completed, making their founder into a saint.

Turning Escriva into a saint is not just an example of how Opus Dei managed to wield its influence. Such a move was important, as it provided Opus Dei with something like a divine blessing. Having its founder be a saint conferred on Opus Dei a huge amount of respect and power within the Catholic Church. The name of Escriva was transformed, changing from the founder of a strange denomination into a one of the Catholic Church's most respected individuals. He is now not only venerated within the Church, but also the Opus Dei founder's name is now a means to an end. With many members happy to pursue a more conservative agenda, the backing of a saint means that Opus Dei could have a big say in the policy of the Catholic Church moving forwards.

By this point, the influence of Opus Dei within the Vatican seems almost confirmed. For an organization of their size, at least, they punch well above their weight. Less than a hundred years old, wielding a large amount of financial muscle, and with the backing of Saint Escriva, they have risen into an unlikely position of influence. When compared to the Jesuits (often labelled as their traditional rivals), one might think that Opus Dei has done exceptionally well to rise to power so quickly. But this section has dwelled on what happens within the Church. What happens when Opus Dei tries to influence the secular world?

Opus Dei has a long history of involvement in conservative politics. It has been a criticism made by many that it has chosen to ally itself with a number of controversial regimes. We've already discussed how Opus Dei has come to resemble the traditionalist, conservative line in Church matters, but this also seems true of its secular activities, even though the organization might deny that there is a cohesive, driven, political effort. But there's a famous saying within the organization, often attributed to Escriva, that says that

"Opus Dei does not act; its members do." Even if the founder was against a single political party, even if members are supposedly independent, there is no denying the influence Opus Dei has had on the world's political stage.

In recent years, for example, Opus Dei has had strong ties with American politicians and one-time Presidential front-runner, Rick Santorum. In the organization's native Spain, Opus Dei members have recently been minister of defense, a national police chief, and a leading financial official. Peruvian congressmen have been Opus Dei members. Italy has had Opus Dei members of parliament. Poland has had leading politicians who have been Opus Dei members. In Chile, it was the mayor of the capital city and the leader of one of the biggest political parties. The two things that they all had in common were Opus Dei membership and a lean towards the conservative side of the spectrum.

One of the best examples of Opus Dei's controversial dalliance with politics is perhaps a result of Escriva's insistence that his Church remain free from such matters. At the end of Spain's fascist era, the Vatican was behind the decision to form a Christian Democratic Party. Escriva outright refused to take part. This has led some people to label him as a fascist sympathizer. To others, the reality was that Escriva both wished to remain isolated from politics and wanted to focus on his mission to have Opus Dei declared a personal prelature. What is true, however, is that the death of Escriva has seen a relaxation in the organization's tendency to take political sides.

As mentioned previously, there is little doubt that Opus Dei's politics lean to the right. This is true both within the church and within secular communities. Their stance on political stalwarts such as gay marriage, abortion, and other right wing viewpoints leaves little doubt on where they stand in a current political climate. This is likely a result of the organization steadfastly refusing to modernize, clinging to the views Escriva imposed on it since the early days. As time passes, Opus Dei is closer towards the far right than ever before. As more and more people begin to see Opus Dei as the religious defendant of many right wing issues, its support will only grow. Even if people do not become members themselves, those of a conservative alignment will offer their support and their backing to an organization that they believe is standing up for the views they share. In that alone, Opus Dei is becoming essentially a political entity. Such an issue leads us neatly into the last section in this guide, in which we hope to answer the question of whether Opus Dei can be accused of being a cult.

Is Opus Dei a Cult?

Most of this book has been leading up to this one question. For many people, hearing about Opus Dei and its sometimes shocking practices can immediately prompt comparisons with other cults. Certainly, listening to ex-members of Opus Dei, there are many stories of cult-like behavior. But the truth is not quite so clear cut.

One of the biggest differences between Opus Dei and the majority of cults is tradition. Looking at most of the Christian-centric cults, most will prompt a turn away from tradition and a move towards new ideas. Opus Dei rigidly clings to traditional beliefs, but it differs from traditional Catholicism. Often, the organization can be said to compromise the freedom of conscience its members possess. Criticisms include allegations of mind control, of breaking apart families, of making it difficult to leave the organization, and that the very existence of Opus Dei harms the Catholic Church.

A key difference between Opus Dei and most cults is the backing it receives from the Vatican. Most cults will be offshoots of organized religion, very rarely operating in tandem with the typical believers. But that does not mean that Opus Dei does not achieve the same results. The allegations of mind control often concern pluralism, of the tendency of all Opus Dei members to eventually sound and appear the same. Once cut off inside the centers, people are said to become like "clones." Combine this with the mortification and the religious devotion, and it's easy to see why the cult comparison is made.

Reports from ex-members describe an unexpected change in conditions once they become members. We mentioned earlier how many of the more extreme mortification tools came as a surprise to numeraries who had just whistled, but even the conditions in the centers themselves are often not adequately explained until it is too late. Even if the Opus Dei centers appear lavish, they often mask harsh living conditions. Many ex-members have said that, if the entirety of their experience had been adequately laid out to them, they would not have joined.

Another cult-like practice involves confession. Members are encouraged to admit their sins in confession, a practice that has fallen out of favor in mainstream

Catholicism. Once they have done so, the priests and Opus Dei members' advise methods of atonement. Psychologically, it can make people dependent on the practice as they look to quell the guilt that the religion induces in them. Furthermore, they are often encouraged to admit their failings in front of a group, something that can be an emotionally harrowing experience. Add in the monitoring of all mail that passes into the center, the limited amount of financial freedom given to members, and a limit on access to all forms of media, and it's easy to see how people get stuck inside the cultish bubble.

In fact, the confession process has been labelled one of the Opus Dei's most troubling practices. Unlike traditional Catholicism, priests are encouraged to keep track of their subject's confessions. In Scientology, this practice has been heavily criticized, with the unmentioned threat that secrets will be released to the public should a person decide to leave the religion. Though this is yet to happen in any large scale with regards to Opus Dei, the implication is certainly present. The organization argues that this is not policy, and that it cannot be found anywhere in the statutes. While this is true, the proliferation of such a practice means that it happens anyway.

Another big issue is money. Numeraries can often contribute up to 22% of their salary to Opus Dei. This includes food, shelter, clothing, and the right to stay in a center. But it also includes donations to the organization and payments for courses and events throughout the year as well as spiritual guidance. It leaves them with little money to spend living anywhere other than a center and often means that they have little in the way of savings. Not only does this make leaving Opus Dei more difficult, but it also means that – come retirement – the numerary is dependent on Opus Dei for assistance.

Perhaps the hallmark of a cult can be how difficult it can be to leave. In Opus Dei, however, there is a relatively large departure rate among those who whistle and then choose not to stay on, estimated at being between 20 and 30 percent, though this number drops significantly as the member progresses deeper into Opus Dei. Leaving is difficult, though. If a member is having doubts, they are warned that departing would be an offence against God. It's a heavy sin to leave the organization, which is especially problematic if those joining are likely to be among the most religious. As well as that, former members have listed constant phone calls, personal visits to the work place and the home, and a flood of letters asking the person to return to Opus Dei. Even allegations of professional sabotage and harassment have been made. For those who have friends only inside the organization, members are encouraged to sever all ties and thus induce a "social death" in the person hoping to leave.

Reports of broken spirits, severed connections, shattered families, and emotional discombobulation for those who try to leave Opus Dei certainly tie in with the issues faced by many people who try to leave cults. The response from the organization itself, however, is that leaving can be incredibly simple. Indeed, before the fidelity stage (i.e. when a person pledges their life to the group), all they have to do to leave is not renew their contract. Opus Dei keeps a register of ex-members who remain on good terms, whose accounts are used to counter balance the negative stories.

It remains difficult to say whether or not Opus Dei is a cult. There is often fine a line between the practices of mainstream religion and niche cults. It is this fine line that Opus Dei often walks down. On some occasions, it leans heavily to one side, while on other occasions, it leans heavily to the other. But it seems to possess the ability to right itself and remain upright at all times. Due to the way in which Opus Dei is now integrated into the Catholic Church, there will often be a backlash against those who attempt to label them as a cult. However, it is certainly more extreme than most mainstream religions. Perhaps it is best to recognize that Opus Dei is unique. This does not make what it does necessarily permissible, nor does it make it evil. But it is important to remain aware of the organization's true nature.

Conclusion

Trying to figure out Opus Dei is an ongoing problem for many people. The organization has gone from strength to strength in a relatively short amount of time, creating a distinct new brand of Catholicism while it does so. In an age when the Church has made a concerted effort to modernize and focus on the poor and disenfranchised, Opus Dei often feels like a throwback to a different era. Its members are conservative, traditional, and possess utter conviction in their beliefs.

Perhaps this is why so many people are so keen to label Opus Dei as a cult. It's no question that its recruiting tactics, its financial strength, and its mortification practices seems completely out of place in our modern society. But you don't have to travel back too far to find a time when this was simply the normal practice for the Catholic Church. That is Opus Dei's greatest strength and its greatest weakness.

Opus Dei reminds us of the cult-like devotion inspired by the world's most popular religion, reminding us of the many centuries when the Church was not quite so sympathetic to the cause of the less fortunate. While this might worry those who do not appreciate the history of Catholicism, there are those who are glad that such a body still exists. Until such time that we're able to resolve this conflict, Opus Dei will not only get more popular, but it will come under increased scrutiny. However, as long as we know the history and the truth about it, we should be in a good place to react to its development.

Further Reading

Agamben, G. (n.d.). *Opus Dei: An Archaeology of Duty.*

Allen, J. (2005). *Opus Dei.* New York: Doubleday.

Allen, J. (2006). *Opus Dei.* London: Penguin.

Escrivá de Balaguer, J. (2006). *The way.* New York: Image/Doubleday.

Hahn, S. (2006). *Ordinary work, extraordinary grace.* New York: Doubleday.

Oates, M., Ruf, L. and Driver, J. (2009). *Women of Opus Dei.* New York: Crossroad Pub. Co.

Tapia, M. (1998). *Beyond the threshold.* New York: Continuum.

Walsh, M. (2004). *Opus Dei.* [San Francisco]: HarperSanFrancisco.

Image Credits

1. Cross of Opus Dei – Creative Commons
2. Tomb of San Josemaria Escrivá de Balaguer - Sergio Calleja
3. Cilice – Creative Commons
4. Opus Dei in the world – Creative Commons
5. Opus Dei's Manhattan Headquarters - Permission was granted through the Opus Dei communications director in the US, Mr. Peter Bancroft
6. The Discipline - travail personnel, photo prise au fr:Musée Unterlinden (Colmar, France)

About the Author

Conrad Bauer is passionate about everything paranormal, unexplained, mysterious, and terrifying. It comes from his childhood and the famous stories his grandfather used to tell the family during summer vacation camping trips. He vividly remembers his grandfather sitting around the fire with new stories to tell everyone who would gather around and listen. His favorites were about the paranormal, including ghost stories, haunted houses, strange places, and paranormal occurrences.

Bauer is an adventurous traveler who has gone to many places in search of the unexplained and paranormal. He has been researching the paranormal and what scares people for more than four decades. He also loves to dig into period of history that are still full of mysteries, being an avid reader of the mystic secret societies that have mark history and remain fascinating and legendary throughout the times. He has accumulated a solid expertise and knowledge that he now shares through his books with his readers and followers.

Conrad, now retired, lives in the countryside in Ireland with his wife and two dogs.

More Books from Conrad Bauer

Just click on the cover to check them out.

HAUNTED
PLACES
CHILLING PARANORMAL AND SUPERNATURAL GHOST STORIES FROM AROUND THE WORLD
CONRAD BAUER

TUNGUSKA
AN APOCALYPTIC EVENT BEYOND BELIEF
CONRAD BAUER

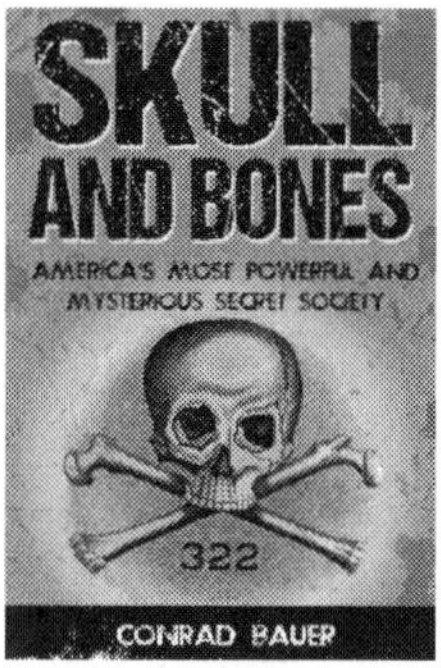
SKULL AND BONES
AMERICA'S MOST POWERFUL AND MYSTERIOUS SECRET SOCIETY
322
CONRAD BAUER

SECRET SOCIETY
The ILLUMINATI
Separating Fact from Fiction
CONRAD BAUER

SHERGAR
A True Crime Story of Kidnapping, Racehorse, and Politics
CONRAD BAUER

HOAX, CONSPIRACY OR SECRET SOCIETY?
The Priory of
SION
Conrad Bauer

Printed in Poland
by Amazon Fulfillment
Poland Sp. z o.o., Wrocław